GOD'S [illegible]CH

ALAN M. STIBBS

INTER-VARSITY PRESS

Inter-Varsity Fellowship
39 Bedford Square, London WC1B 3EY

First Edition May 1959
Reprinted October 1963
Reprinted March 1968
Reprinted April 1973

ISBN 0 85110 501 7

Printed in Great Britain
by Unwin Brothers Limited
The Gresham Press, Old Woking, Surrey, England
A member of the Staples Printing Group

CONTENTS

FOREWORD

MY dominant aim in preparing this survey has been to expound what the Scriptures teach, and thus to trace the sequence of the biblical doctrine of the people of God and to show its coherence. In doing this I have also sought to give prominence to points which are directly relevant to the present condition of the churches, and to expose as such some current ideas about the Church which (at least as I see it) are unscriptural. On issues concerning which the Scriptures seem to me to give no explicit authoritative guidance I have not attempted to discuss the relative merits of the different traditional attitudes and practices. I hope that this study may in consequence be of the more general value to all evangelical Christians.

I am very conscious that I owe much to many teachers and writers who have helped me the better to understand what the Bible teaches on this subject. I am particularly conscious that, in the preparation of this survey, I have owed most to the overruling providence of God, and to the gracious illumination of His Spirit. May He help many who read these pages, as He has helped me in writing them, to a fresher and fuller awareness of what He has revealed for our learning in the written Word concerning His purpose in Christ to have a people to be His very own.

ALAN M. STIBBS

I. OLD TESTAMENT PREPARATION

CHAPTER ONE

GOD'S PURPOSE

GOD made man for Himself. The chief end of God in the creation of man was to have a people of whom He could say: I am theirs, and they are Mine. I will be their God, and they shall be My people. The remarkable story of the Bible is the story of the way in which God still continued with this purpose after, and in spite of, man's fall into sin. In the Bible we learn how, in a fallen and sinful world, in and through earthly history, God is still forming for Himself a people, a people to whom He is pleased to give Himself and the enjoyment of His abiding presence as their God. There is in Scripture no phrase more frequent or more fundamental in its disclosure of the divine mind than variations of the declaration: 'I will be to them a God, and they shall be to me a people.'[1] Also, in the closing chapters of Revelation (to me it is significant that we should find this in what is the concluding section of the whole canon of Scripture) we are given a final vision and assurance of fulfilment. There the inspired seer testifies:

> And I John saw the holy city, new Jerusalem, coming down from God out of heaven, prepared as a bride adorned for her husband. And I heard a great voice out of heaven saying, Behold, the tabernacle of God is with men, and he will dwell with them, and they shall be his people, and God himself shall be with them, and be their God.[2]

Here an illustration may help; and the obvious one to introduce is that of the marriage relationship. For marriage relationship language is used figuratively in the Bible itself for this very purpose of illustrating the character and the intimacy of the relationship between God and men. It is used above in the Scripture just quoted. It is used in the Old Testament of the

[1] See e.g. Ex. vi. 7; Lv. xxvi. 12; Je. xxx. 22; Ezk. xi. 20

[2] Rev. xxi. 2, 3

relationship between God and His people Israel.[1] It is used in the New Testament of the relationship between Christ and His Church.[2]

In the establishment of the marriage relationship, a man freely chooses to invite a woman to become his, and offers to give himself to become hers. In response he demands from her that, in a special and an exclusive way, 'forsaking all other', she should acknowledge him as hers, and give herself to be his. The illustration thus afforded is, in addition, still more appropriate to our purpose, because among us it is customary for such an intention on the part of a man and a woman towards each other to be solemnly declared and sealed in the marriage vow and covenant. In this contract each openly declares to the other, 'I take you to be mine. I give myself to be yours.' Henceforth they can be described or introduced with reference to each other—he as her husband, and she as his wife.

So it is in the relationship between God and His people. Notice for example that He sometimes introduced Himself as 'the God of Abraham';[3] and Abraham was described as 'the Friend of God'.[4] For, as a man chooses a bride and voluntarily invites a woman to become his, so we find that God has freely acted, according to His own will and pleasure. It is He who chooses to say to the children of Israel, 'I will take you to me for a people, and I will be to you a God.'[5] 'I will walk among you, and will be your God, and ye shall be my people.'[6]

Furthermore, God has solemnly and repeatedly pledged Himself in covenant. For example, in addition to the 'covenant which he made with them in Horeb', Moses called upon the Israelites, when they were in the land of Moab, to stand before the Lord:

> That thou shouldest enter into covenant with the Lord thy God, and into his oath, which the Lord thy God maketh with thee this day: that he may establish thee to day for a people unto himself, and that he may be unto thee a God, as he hath said unto thee, and as he hath sworn unto thy fathers.[7]

[1] See Is. liv. 5; Ho. ii. 16, 19, 20
[2] See Eph. v. 23-32
[3] See Gn. xxviii. 13; Ex. iii. 6
[4] See Is. xli. 8; Jas. ii. 23
[5] Ex. vi. 7
[6] Lv. xxvi. 12
[7] Dt. xxix. 1, 10-13

It was in such divine confirmation of God's choice of them, and of their corporate relation to Him, that national leaders like Samuel and David later found assurance and hope.[1] Inspired prophets also spoke repeatedly of a coming fuller realization of this divine intention. God would make a new covenant to further this very end.

> This shall be the covenant that I will make with the house of Israel; After those days, saith the Lord, I will put my law in their inward parts, and write it in their hearts; and will be their God, and they shall be my people.[2]

This was explicitly the larger hope of the future.

> Behold, I will save my people from the east country, and from the west country; and I will bring them, and they shall dwell in the midst of Jerusalem: and they shall be my people, and I will be their God, in truth and in righteousness.[3]

Also, it was foreseen that this would involve bringing into this privileged relationship those who had previously been complete outsiders; so we read that the Lord saith:

> I will say to them which were not my people, Thou art my people; and they shall say, Thou art my God.[4]

And the full significance of such words is indicated and underlined by their quotation in the New Testament.[5]

On the other hand, it was equally clearly indicated that full enjoyment on man's part of this relation to God demanded personal separation from every inconsistent attachment in order to be wholly and exclusively His. To further this end disciplinary divine judgments were seen to be necessary to remove the unworthy, and to bring men to repentance and obedience.

> And it shall come to pass, that in all the land, saith the Lord, two parts therein shall be cut off and die; but the third shall be left therein. And I will bring the third part through the fire, and will refine them as silver is refined, and will try them as gold is tried: they shall call on my name, and I will hear them; I will say, It is my people: and they shall say, the Lord is my God.[6]

[1] See 1 Sa. xii. 22; 2 Sa. vii. 24; 1 Ch. xvii. 22
[2] Je. xxxi. 33; cf. Ezk. xxxvi. 25-28, xxxvii. 26, 27
[3] Zc. viii. 7, 8
[4] Ho. ii. 23, cf. i. 10
[5] See Rom. ix. 25, 26; 1 Pet. ii. 10
[6] Zc. xiii. 8, 9; cf. Je. vii. 23

Similarly, in the day of larger fulfilment in Christ, men enjoying the knowledge of the gospel are urged by the apostle, 'Be ye not unequally yoked together with unbelievers', and 'Come out from among them, and be ye separate', in order that they may enter into the realized experience of all that God has both promised and made possible in Christ. Nor can the inspired New Testament writer better express this intended destiny set before us Christians than by quoting the familiar Old Testament language. So Paul says:

> For ye are the temple of the living God; as God hath said, I will dwell in them, and walk in them; and I will be their God, and they shall be my people.[1]

It is, therefore, God's unmistakable purpose to have a people of His own; and by His amazing grace it is the utterly undeserved privilege of all who belong to Christ to belong to this community, the people of God. It is the character and outworking of this purpose and this privilege that we are now to study.

God revealed what was in His mind, and how He purposed to fulfil it, by what He did. Here the Old Testament Scriptures have for men of every age and race an abiding relevance and importance. Not only do they record the beginnings of God's action; they also show—as the subsequent witness of the New Testament explicitly confirms—that in these initial stages God, in His providence and by His Spirit, deliberately acted in such a way as to prepare men's minds for the proper appreciation of the ultimate fulfilment of His purpose in Christ. So we find that in the Old Testament record of God's special dealings with a chosen people, a pattern reveals itself which is indicative of the governing principles and of the successive stages of the divine plan. Let us briefly survey its outstanding features.

In the Old Testament, the history of God's chosen people begins with God's choice and call of Abraham. Here the initiative is wholly God's. He acts in sovereign grace according

[1] See 2 Cor. vi. 14–18

to His own predetermined pleasure and to fulfil His own predestined end. He selects whom He pleases, and invites him to forsake all else and everyone else in order to follow Him, and to enjoy His rewards. So we read that to Abraham the Lord said:

> Get thee out of thy country, and from thy kindred, and from thy father's house, unto a land that I will shew thee: and I will make of thee a great nation, and I will bless thee, and make thy name great; and thou shalt be a blessing.[1]

This movement of God in special relation to one chosen individual can be described more technically or theologically—first, as His 'election' and 'predestination' of Abraham, and second, as His 'calling' of Abraham. All membership in God's chosen people depends primarily upon similar divine action—first, upon God's election and predestination, and second, upon God's calling.[2] Also this initial movement of God towards Abraham indicates and emphasizes that God elects and calls men individually, by name, one by one, into intimate personal relationship with Himself. In the ultimate vast community of God's people, therefore, every individual member is meant similarly to be sure of his own personal election and calling.[3]

When God thus said in effect to Abraham, 'I want you,—to be Mine', He also equally said to Abraham, by unmistakable implication, 'You shall have Me. I will be *your* God.' To this invitation Abraham responded. So we read that Abraham 'called upon the name of the Lord'.[4] This also is, both theologically and biblically, very significant phraseology. It means that Abraham began to acknowledge and to invoke God in an intimate personal way as *his* God. Such phraseology becomes in the Bible a familiar way of describing, from the side of human response, all who belong to God and are members of His people. They are those who 'call upon the name of the Lord'.[5] It is in these terms that the prophet Joel describes those

[1] Gn. xii. 1, 2

[2] See Rom. viii. 28–30, ix. 11, 24, xi. 5; Gal. i. 15; 1 Thes. i. 4; 2 Pet. i. 10

[3] See again Gal. i. 15; 2 Pet. i. 10

[4] Gn. xii. 8

[5] See Zp. iii. 9

whom God will save in the coming day of deliverance. 'And it shall come to pass, that whosoever shall call on the name of the Lord shall be delivered.'[1] It is also in such terms that, in the New Testament, the apostle Paul describes the members of the universal Church as 'all that in every place call upon the name of Jesus Christ our Lord'.[2]

Thus in God's dealings with Abraham, and in Abraham's characteristic response to God, we see the two complementary activities which bring God and men together into fellowship. First, God calls men individually to be His; and then they, in response, call upon His name, and acknowledge Him as theirs.

When we move on in the Old Testament story to the book of Exodus, we find that it complements the witness of the book of Genesis. It records the outworked fulfilment of God's purpose, which was begun in His choice and call of Abraham. Here we see God dealing, not with a single individual only, but with a whole community, the nation of the Israelites. Here, significantly, we are made aware of the place and necessity of redemption. For the people whom God has chosen to be His are seen to be in bondage in a foreign land. So, before they could fully become God's people, and belong only to Him, they had to be redeemed. Thus we read that God said to them:

> I will bring you out from under the burdens of the Egyptians . . . and I will redeem you with a stretched out arm, and with great judgments: and I will take you to me for a people, and I will be to you a God.[3]

And after the Israelites went out from Egypt, and had crossed the Red Sea, they sang, 'Thou in thy mercy hast led forth the people which thou hast redeemed.'[4] Also, it is in Exodus xii, in the story of the Passover, that the words first appear in Scripture which are translated 'the whole assembly of the congregation'.[5] The two Hebrew nouns of this phrase provide the antecedents of the more familiar Greek words, which we

[1] Joel ii. 32
[2] 1 Cor. i. 2
[3] Ex. vi. 6, 7
[4] Ex. xv. 13
[5] Ex. xii. 6

know as 'ecclesia' and 'synagogue'. It is surely very significant indeed that the Lord's assembly or 'ecclesia', His Church or congregation, is first spoken of as constituted when the Israelites were called together under the Passover blood to eat the Passover lamb. This, indeed, was a night to be much remembered by Israelites, 'a night to be much observed unto the Lord for bringing them out from the land of Egypt'.[1] It was the night of their birth or emergence as God's people. So we find later that the psalmist prayed:

> Remember thy congregation, which thou hast purchased of old; the rod of thine inheritance, which thou hast redeemed.[2]

This idea finds its obvious Christian counterpart and fulfilment in the redemption which Jesus wrought, when He was 'sacrificed for us' as 'our passover'.[3] For through His death and resurrection He accomplished 'an exodus' for the Israel of God. (Such is the phraseology used by Luke to describe the subject of our Lord's conversation with Moses and Elijah on the Mount of Transfiguration.[4]) So in Paul's Epistle to Titus we read of Christ that He

> gave himself for us, that he might redeem us from all iniquity, and purify unto himself a peculiar people (RV, 'a people for his own possession').[5]

The New Testament fulfilment is thus described in words which re-echo the language of the Old Testament figure or preparatory pattern. So, just as the psalmist of Old Testament times prayed, 'Remember thy congregation, which thou hast purchased',[6] so the apostle of the New Testament days spoke of 'the church of God, which he hath purchased with his own blood'.[7]

In the third place, let us notice from both Genesis and Exodus that these approaches of God to men in grace to make them His, and to offer Himself to be theirs, and to promise them His blessings, were also confirmed by the visible seals of a

[1] Ex. xii. 42
[2] Ps. lxxiv. 2
[3] See 1 Cor. v. 7
[4] See Lk. ix. 30, 31
[5] Tit. ii. 14
[6] Ps. lxxiv. 2
[7] Acts xx. 28

properly ordered covenant; that is, one duly ratified by the performance of the customary ritual. This, says the writer to the Hebrews, is how men make their fellows doubly sure. Having given their word, they confirm it by oath.[1] Such oath-taking and covenant-making commonly involve either invoking God's name or introducing visible pledges. So, for instance, in the form of marriage used in the Church of England, in addition to the mutual promises which both the man and the woman make, the divine Name is invoked by the man, and a ring is given by the man and received by the woman, in token and pledge of the vow and covenant made between them.

In His dealings with Abraham we read that God said:

> I will establish my covenant between me and thee and thy seed after thee . . . to be a God unto thee, and to thy seed after thee. . . . This is my covenant, which ye shall keep. . . . Every man child among you shall be circumcised . . . and it shall be a token of the covenant betwixt me and you.[2]

Circumcision was, therefore, a sign and seal put upon each male Israelite's body, that God had pledged Himself to be their God, and intended them to be His people. It was a necessary and decisive visible mark indicating membership, first, in Abraham's household,[3] and later, within the nation of the Israelites. For instance, we are later told concerning participation in the ordinance of the passover that 'All the congregation of Israel shall keep it', but that 'no uncircumcised person shall eat thereof'.[4]

In addition, God assured Abraham that his seed should inherit the land of Canaan by introducing the symbolism of putting to death. The pieces or rent parts of slain animals were divided, half on one side, and half on the other, and the light, which symbolized God's presence, passed between them.[5] It seems probable that when men sealed a covenant by thus passing (or by referring to the practice of thus passing) between the divided parts of slain animals, they said, as they made

[1] See Heb. vi. 16–18
[2] Gn. xvii. 7, 10, 11
[3] See Gn. xvii. 12, 13, 27
[4] Ex. xii. 47, 48
[5] See Gn. xv. 7–21

their promise or vow, 'the Lord do so to me, and more also'; that is, may God treat me as these animals have been treated, if I fail to keep my word.[1] This practice may be compared to a man swearing 'upon his life', and perhaps drawing a knife across his throat as he does so, that is, using the symbolism of putting to death. Similarly, at Sinai, Moses sacrificed oxen and sprinkled half of the blood on the altar, and sprinkled the rest of the blood on the people, and said, 'Behold the blood of the covenant, which the Lord hath made with you.'[2] Thus, by adopting familiar human usage, God assured Abraham and the Israelites that they were indeed to be His people, and to enjoy the fulfilment of His promises.

Such awareness may perhaps set us on the road to a fuller biblical understanding of the appointed place and purpose in the household of God and in the congregation of Christ of the two so-called sacraments of the gospel: baptism and the Lord's supper. For they, too, confirm God's words of promise. They are seals of God's covenant with His people. In baptism God's name is invoked, and a visible seal put upon the individual's body. Thus are God's promises, to make us His, visibly signed and sealed. In the Lord's supper, on the other hand, 'the pieces' used to remind us of Christ's sacrifice are visibly divided. At the institution in the upper room there was a deliberate interval between the breaking of the bread and the handing round of the cup. It was not until 'he had supped' that Jesus 'took the cup'.[3] So, says the apostle, 'as often as ye eat this bread, and drink this cup', what you proclaim is the Lord's death.[4] Also, when Jesus thus 'divided the pieces' and 'took the cup' in His hand, He immediately spoke of 'the new covenant'.[5] It is, therefore, 'by these presents', by the uttered word and the added visible seal, that in receiving the sacraments we are meant to be assured that we are God's people, and that He and all His promised benefits are ours.

[1] See Je. xxxiv. 18–20; Ru. i. 17; 2 Ki. vi. 31
[2] See Ex. xxiv. 3–8; Heb. ix. 18–20
[3] See 1 Cor. xi. 25
[4] See 1 Cor. xi. 26 and RV
[5] See 1 Cor. xi. 25 and RV

CHAPTER TWO

THE VISIBLE AND THE TRUE ISRAEL

IN the Old Testament story, God's chosen people, first the household of Abraham, and later the nation of the Israelites, form a distinct and visibly recognizable community. Such distinction was made the more unmistakable by outward marks which all could recognize, such as belonging by birth to the seed of Abraham, being circumcised, and joining in the public and regular acknowledgement of God, for example by calling upon the name of the Lord, keeping the weekly sabbath, and observing the annual ordinance of the Passover. By such marks as these it was easy for others to distinguish Israelites, and to know whether any individual did, or did not, belong to them. Also, this distinct community was equally clearly the community with which God in providence and grace had special dealings. It was the sphere in which He particularly manifested His presence, and worked to further His special pre-determined purposes.

Yet from the Old Testament story it is equally plain that, within this clearly-defined, visible community, a further distinction is frequently to be made between nominal and actual membership, between the professing and the true people of God. As it is put by the apostle Paul: 'They are not all Israel, which are of Israel.'[1] In other words, not all who belong to the visible community are genuine Israelites.

Also, while the witness of Scripture compels us to recognize the presence of this further distinction, it is not possible in the same decisive way, from evidence immediately open to the senses, to know where the dividing line comes, or to which class any particular individual may belong. For the true seed is to be recognized primarily by faith rather than by sight, and the essential characteristics of a true Israelite are funda-

[1] Rom. ix. 6

mentally inward rather than outward. So this distinct community of true Israelites, because it is not discernible by the senses, particularly by sight, has by some been called, in contrast to the outwardly visible community, a spiritual or 'invisible' community, whose membership is exactly known only to God.

This inevitable distinction between the visible and the true is, in principle, still one of great relevance to the community of God's people, which is to be found in the Church of Christ. It is worthy of careful, detailed attention, therefore, particularly as there is so much to be learnt about it from the Bible itself. Here, too, we are not left to our own judgment. We have the inspired and apostolic guidance of the New Testament to help us to arrive at a proper Christian understanding of the witness of the Old Testament. There are in the Epistles several passages of pointed comment on Old Testament history, indicating its abiding significance for the people of God.

Let us start with the household of Abraham. Here all the members belonged to the distinct visible community; and so, when circumcision was introduced as a token of God's covenant with Abraham and his seed, all the males were circumcised.

> In the selfsame day was Abraham circumcised, and Ishmael his son. And all the men of his house, born in the house, and bought with money of the stranger, were circumcised with him.[1]

Yet, this is how St. Paul comments:

> Neither, because they are the seed of Abraham, are they all children: but, In Isaac shall thy seed be called.[2] That is, They which are the children of the flesh, these are not the children of God: but the children of the promise are counted for the seed.[3]

So, among the members of Abraham's household, Isaac only was the true seed, and his identity was not distinguishable by sight, but known only to faith. What secured for Isaac participation in the inheritance was not just physical descent from

[1] Gn. xvii. 26, 27 [2] Quoted from Gn. xxi. 12 [3] Rom. ix. 7, 8

Abraham and circumcision, by themselves, for Ishmael had both of these. Rather it was what he possessed in addition, the election and promise of God, and a divinely-wrought, supernatural birth.

Let us look further at the significance of circumcision. On the one hand, circumcision was the indispensable condition of membership in the visible community of God's people. 'Every man child' we read, 'must needs be circumcised', or 'be cut off from his people'.[1] Yet, in his Epistle to the Romans, Paul argues that the essential gospel blessing of justification before God, of having righteousness instead of sin reckoned to his account, was enjoyed by Abraham through faith alone before he was circumcised. Circumcision was added as a sign and seal of a blessing enjoyed. The blessing came, not through circumcision, but through faith. This means, says St. Paul, that others can, without sharing his circumcision, become Abraham's true spiritual descendants and share his blessing, if they share Abraham's faith; and that those who do share Abraham's circumcision will become true children of Abraham and share his blessing only if they share his faith.[2]

To put it in other words, as St. Paul had already done in this same Epistle to the Romans, this means that the true Israelite, the genuine member of God's people, is not the perfect, visible conformist, who has properly shared outwardly in the divinely-ordained rite of initiation, but the man who makes unseen and sincere heart response to God and His ways.

> For he is not a Jew, which is one outwardly; neither is that circumcision, which is outward in the flesh: but he is a Jew, which is one inwardly; and circumcision is that of the heart, in the spirit, and not in the letter; whose praise is not of men, but of God.[3]

One way to reckon the people of God is to reckon them as seen by men, according to what is visible. This community is, however, always mixed, not pure. 'In the visible Church the evil be ever mingled with the good.'[4] The right way to reckon

[1] Gn. xvii. 12–14 [2] See Rom. iv. 9–12 [3] Rom. ii. 28, 29
[4] *XXXIX Articles*, Art. xxvi

the true people of God is by faith, to reckon them as seen by God.

> For the Lord seeth not as man seeth; for man looketh on the outward appearance, but the Lord looketh on the heart.[1]

These things thus 'written aforetime' in the Old Testament were, as St. Paul also says in the same Epistle to the Romans, 'written for our learning'.[2] They have their obvious Christian application. For instance, while it is proper for professing Christians to be baptized, since baptism is the divinely-ordained seal of membership in the visible Church, in God's sight the true children of Abraham are not the baptized as such, but the believers in Christ. Those, upon whom 'the blessing of Abraham' comes, are those who 'receive the promise of the Spirit through faith'.[3]

It is very necessary, therefore, in all our thinking about God's people to make a proper distinction between the nominal and the genuine, between the professing and the real, members; between the outer or larger containing company, those outwardly associated with the things of God, and the inner and true elect community, those who know the Lord; between what Richard Hooker and others, both before and since, have called the visible and the invisible Church, between the formal or sacramental membership able to be numbered by men, and the deeper spiritual membership fully known only to God.

Let us think next of the exodus of the Israelites from Egypt. In writing to Christians, St. Paul, when he mentions them, calls all 'our fathers'. He recalls that these Israelites all shared outwardly and visibly in the signs and seals of membership in God's people. In a word, as St. Paul explicitly emphasizes, they all shared in direct counterparts of the Christian sacraments. Yet they were not all pleasing to God. Many of them were overthrown in the wilderness. Though, on the other hand, it is equally important to remember that their failure was not complete. There was a remnant of faith. Joshua and

[1] 1 Sa. xvi. 7 [2] Rom. xv. 4 [3] See Gal. iii. 14

Caleb did enter the promised land. Let us quote and consider the apostle's exact words:

> Moreover, brethren, I would not that ye should be ignorant, how that all our fathers were under the cloud, and all passed through the sea; and were all baptized unto Moses in the cloud and in the sea; and did all eat the same spiritual meat; and did all drink the same spiritual drink: for they drank of that spiritual Rock that followed them: and that Rock was Christ. But with many of them God was not well pleased: for they were overthrown in the wilderness.[1]

These apostolic words, intended in their context as a solemn warning to professing Christians, plainly imply that in the visible community of the Israelites, all of whom shared outwardly and equally in God's mighty deliverance of them from Egypt, the majority failed to prove themselves true members of God's chosen people. Their hearts were not right with God.

The same evidence is similarly used as a warning in the Epistle to the Hebrews. The writer quotes, as the present utterance of the Spirit ('as the Holy Ghost saith'[2]), the inspired witness of Psalm xcv. He thus reminds his readers concerning those who 'came out of Egypt by Moses', that to many of them God sware in His wrath, 'They shall not enter into my rest.'[3] So they failed to enter in. This also unmistakably implies that God disowned them as His people. The writer of the Epistle asks why, and draws the explicit conclusion that it was because of their own unbelief and disobedience. 'So we see', he writes, 'that they could not enter in because of unbelief.'[4]

We thus learn once again the same lesson, this time with more positive reference to the underlying spiritual cause. The one visible community, composed of individuals who are all temporarily united, not only by participation in distinctive religious ceremonies, but also by actual experience of the benefits of God's saving power, is seen ultimately to be divided by causes which are not in the same way immediately visible and distinguishable, namely the inner responsive faith, or the rebellious unbelief, of the individual heart and

[1] I Cor. x. 1–5 [2] Heb. iii. 7 [3] See Heb. iii. 10, 11, 16 [4] Heb. iii. 19

will.[1] In this way the scriptural record of the Israelites journeying through the wilderness illustrates clearly (and the later witness of the New Testament drives it home as of abiding application) that final entrance into the predestined inheritance of the people of God belongs not to the visibly present, nor to the outwardly proper (as such), but to the inwardly true. What matters, what in the end becomes decisive, is genuine heart faith and diligent practical obedience; and these are always characteristically found in some, but not in all, of the visible community.

Thus, in our study of God's people in the Old Testament, we may begin to discern the emergence of the idea of a spiritual fellowship or faithful remnant, a company of heart-believers eager to obey God's word, a true Church whose membership is visible only to God, existing within the containing nation or visible Church here on earth, that is, within the larger company immediately distinguishable by men, who by their common activities and characteristics bear all the proper outward marks and sacramental signs of Church membership.

According to the Scriptures of both Old and New Testaments, it is this faithful remnant who are God's true people. So St. Paul, appealing to the witness of the Old Testament, says of his own day, and more generally of the Christian era, 'Even so then at this present time also there is a remnant according to the election of grace.'[2] For instance, to use the illustration to which the apostle appeals, in Elijah's day we find witness borne by God to the existence of such a remnant. Because of the spread of Baal worship in Israel, Elijah thought that he was the only one left faithful to Jehovah. 'I, even I only, am left',[3] he said. But God answered:

> Yet I have left me seven thousand in Israel, all the knees which have not bowed unto Baal, and every mouth which hath not kissed him.[4]

[1] See e.g. Heb. iii. 12

[2] Rom. xi. 5; see also verses 2–4; Is. i. 9, x. 20–23, xi. 11, 16, xxxvii. 31, 32, etc.

[3] 1 Ki. xix. 10

[4] 1 Ki. xix. 18

These seven thousand faithful souls were not, as such, visible to men or able to be numbered by men. They were fully and exactly known only to God.

Similarly, in his own day, when St. Paul was painfully aware that false teachers had overthrown the faith of some, he added in faith, and not by sight:

> Nevertheless the foundation of God standeth sure, having this seal, The Lord knoweth them that are his.[1]

In this connection, therefore, in addition to holding fast to this confidence, it is important that we should be humble enough to recognize that neither we, nor the Church—not even her leaders, like Elijah—can always tell who or how many the faithful are. Thus in a very decisive sense the exact membership of the true Church of God is invisible to men.

Again, in Isaiah's day, when before the threat of invasion the Israelites were tending to trust in foreign alliances rather than in God, Isaiah gathered around him a company of disciples, bound by trust in the Lord and by loyalty to His word.[2] Here the nominal and the faithful in Israel become more openly and visibly distinguished, because, in a day of unbelief and apostasy on the part of those publicly known as God's people, the faithful remnant, or some of them, form a separate distinct congregation and make a public confession. So we find Isaiah saying:

> Bind up the testimony, seal the law among my disciples. And I will wait upon the Lord, that hideth his face from the house of Jacob, and I will look for him. Behold, I and the children whom the Lord hath given me are for signs and for wonders in Israel from the Lord of hosts, which dwelleth in mount Zion. And when they shall say unto you, Seek unto them that have familiar spirits, . . . To the law and to the testimony: if they speak not according to this word, it is because there is no light in them.[3]

What we see happening here is, in principle, a movement sometimes necessarily repeated since in the history of the Church of Christ. It was, for instance, over against a corrupt Church, and not over against the godless world, that the Reformers of the sixteenth century made their appeal to the

[1] See 2 Tim. ii. 16–19 [2] See Is. viii. 5–20 [3] Is. viii. 16–20

Bible, drew up confessions of faith, and formed separate, distinct congregations. It is noteworthy, also, that when Isaiah thus rallied the faithful few, the criterion to which he appealed by which to distinguish truth from error, and light from darkness, was the God-given law and testimony. Here, in principle, is the abiding court of appeal by which to expose and oppose wrong teaching, by which to justify necessary separation and independent meeting together, and by which to settle all matters of faith and conduct, namely the plain injunction and witness of the God-given Word.

Later still in the Old Testament story, when the children of Israel were in exile in Babylon, it was only a minority, a company inspired and bound together not merely by racial kinship and patriotic zeal, but rather by faith in and devotion to Jehovah, who responded to the challenge to return to Jerusalem, and rebuild the temple. If the exile was national, a captivity of the Jewish race, the return was religious, a movement of the more spiritually-minded. So do the very crises and challenges of history and circumstances serve, under God's providence, to force into open expression the deep underlying distinction between the nominal and the true in the visible community of the Israel of God.

Subsequent to all this, the Jews of the Dispersion, scattered in many lands outside Palestine, came widely to welcome into their synagogue meetings for worship, and even into full fellowship in the Passover, as members of Jehovah's people, proselytes from among the Gentile nations. These happenings and developments all served to make it increasingly plain that membership in the true Israel was not merely a racial heritage, or a simple consequence of ritual participation in distinctive ceremonies, but rather a personal and individual affair, a matter of spiritual condition and of heart response, something, therefore, in principle open equally to men and women of all races. So, by becoming at first more restricted to the faithful minority, it was already showing itself to be capable of extension to men of every nation under heaven. It is such further restriction and extension that we must consider in more detail in the following chapters.

CHAPTER THREE

VISIONS OF THE CITY OF GOD

THE Old Testament story frequently implies, and New Testament comment explicitly confirms, that, when men truly respond in the obedience of faith to the call and promise of God, possibilities are set before them to be embraced which far exceed the limits of what is visible here and now, and indeed transcends all that is temporal and earthly. For such faith in God, in His Word and work, becomes 'the substance of things hoped for, the evidence of things not seen'.[1] It gives men conviction concerning the certainties of the unseen and the future, of the eternal and the heavenly. This, too, was the kind of new awareness into which God deliberately led the pioneers of faith, whose progress and triumphs the Scriptures record. May God help us also, by His Word and Spirit, to enter more into the same kind of spiritual discovery and enrichment.

When Abraham believed that God would give him the seed to possess the land,[2] he embraced a hope beyond the natural promise of his personal circumstances. For his wife Sarah (and this is, significantly, the first thing recorded of her in the Bible) 'was barren; she had no child'.[3] To quote Paul's comments: Over against 'the deadness of Sarah's womb' Abraham set faith in 'God, who quickeneth the dead'.[4] So Isaac was born; by God's doing. This indicates what becomes in Scripture as a whole the governing principle in the emergence and increase of the people of God's purpose, those who are to possess the predestined inheritance. The members of this community are not just born naturally 'of the flesh'. They must be born supernaturally 'of the Spirit',[5] by the special intervention of God. In its larger, Christian fulfilment this is

[1] Heb. xi. 1
[2] See Gn. xii. 7
[3] Gn. xi. 30
[4] See Rom. iv. 17–21
[5] See Jn. iii. 5–8

prophetically anticipated by Isaiah in a passage which, significantly, follows the crucial fifty-third chapter:

> Sing, O barren, thou that didst not bear; break forth into singing, and cry aloud, thou that didst not travail with child: for more are the children of the desolate than the children of the married wife, saith the Lord. . . . For thou shalt break forth on the right hand and on the left; and thy seed shall inherit the Gentiles, and make the desolate cities to be inhabited . . . For thy Maker is thine husband; the Lord of hosts is his name.[1]

When Abraham was confronted by the demand to offer up Isaac, his faith made further progress. He believed that God would provide not only the necessary sacrifice,[2] but also, as it seemed, the necessary resurrection of Isaac from the dead.[3] Again, such faith was, in principle, laying hold of truth beyond the immediate limits of human resource and experience. For the ultimate raising up by God of the seed to possess the inheritance does depend upon God's own prior provision of the atoning sacrifice of the Lamb of God, and upon His resurrection of Christ from the dead. So, in some real sense, Abraham, by faith, rejoiced to see Christ's day.[4] Also, out of such a heart-searching experience of God's ways, he learnt, by faith, to look for divine fulfilment beyond the possibilities of the earthly and the temporal, and beyond the limits of man's short life in this world. So when, as far as the earthly land of promise was concerned, he still dwelt in it as in a foreign country, he nevertheless 'by faith' still 'looked for a city which hath foundations, whose builder and maker is God'.[5] Thus he, and those who followed his faith,

> all died in faith, not having received the promises, but having seen them afar off, and were persuaded of them, and embraced them, and confessed that they were strangers and pilgrims on the earth.[6]

So, through such discipline, and by such enlarged faith, they became those of whom it is witnessed: 'But now they desire a better country, that is, an heavenly: wherefore' (and let us

[1] See Is. liv. 1–5; cf. also verse 13
[2] Gn. xxii. 8
[3] Heb. xi. 17–19
[4] See Gn. xxii. 14; Jn. viii. 56
[5] Heb. xi. 9, 10
[6] Heb. xi. 13

notice the significance of this comment) 'God is not ashamed to be called their God: for he hath prepared for them a city.'[1]

Thus we may discern, by the aid of the insight of the inspired New Testament writer, the true goal of God's promises to Abraham, Isaac and Jacob. They were not called in order to become merely the ancestors of an earthly nation who should possess in Palestine an earthly mother-country as their own. Rather, God's purpose was that they themselves should be brought, together with all their spiritual seed, to the heavenly city, where above and beyond all else they are to be God's people, and openly to enjoy Him as *their God*. When the Israelites were delivered from bondage in Egypt, and led through the wilderness into Canaan, the Bible record ultimately makes plain that God had for them a goal in view beyond the territorial possession of Palestine. For instance, of those who hardened their hearts, and turned from God in unbelief in the wilderness, it is not only written, that the Lord sware, saying:

> Surely there shall not one of these men of this evil generation see that good land, which I sware to give unto your fathers, save Caleb. . . . (and) Joshua.[2]

These people are also those of whom God says,

> Unto whom I sware in my wrath that they should not enter into my rest.[3]

The full goal in view, therefore, was spiritual rather than physical, namely entrance into the rest or 'sabbath' of God. It is to this spiritual fulfilment that the writer to the Hebrews devotes the whole of his attention, as the true goal of the promise and purpose of God for His people.[4]

Also, when the Israelites had occupied most of the promised land, a further purpose of God is given prominence and priority, namely His purpose to choose out one special, unique place to put His name there, and to manifest His presence, so that it might become the place to which all the Israelites from all over the land would regularly go up to appear together before the Lord. The crowning glory of God's purpose for

[1] Heb. xi. 16 [2] Dt. i. 34–38 [3] Ps. xcv. 11 [4] See Heb. iv. 1, 6–11

them is thus shown to be not just the enjoyment of a territorial inheritance but being gathered in His presence as His people. So we read:

> Three times in a year shall all thy males appear before the Lord thy God in the place which he shall choose.[1]

For the realization of this purpose God chose out mount Zion. This was the one place in the land which was to become known as 'the city of our God',[2] or, as our Lord called it, 'the city of the great King',[3] in whose palaces 'God is known . . . for a refuge.'[4] So we read:

> Moreover he refused the tabernacle of Joseph, and chose not the tribe of Ephraim: but chose the tribe of Judah, the mount Zion which he loved.[5]
>
> The Lord loveth the gates of Zion more than all the dwellings of Jacob. Glorious things are spoken of thee, O city of God.[6]
>
> For the Lord hath chosen Zion; he hath desired it for his habitation.[7]

The fulfilment of this purpose was not possible until David captured Jerusalem and took possession of mount Zion as its king.[8] Here it was that David not only set his own throne or palace, but he also set God's tabernacle. So we read:

> And they brought in the ark of the Lord, and set it in his place, in the midst of the tabernacle that David had pitched for it.[9]

In this connection David's Psalms reveal his twofold concern; first, that this might be God's dwelling-place, His tabernacle, His holy hill, and, second, that His people might be fit there to ascend and to abide. So he asks:

> Lord, who shall abide in thy tabernacle? who shall dwell in thy holy hill?[10]
>
> Who shall ascend into the hill of the Lord? or who shall stand in his holy place?[11]

Such awareness was used to enable David prophetically to anticipate in these very terms God's larger purpose in Christ.

[1] Dt. xvi. 16
[2] Ps. xlviii. 1, 8
[3] Mt. v. 35
[4] See Ps. xlviii. 2, 3
[5] Ps. lxxviii. 67, 68
[6] Ps. lxxxvii. 2, 3
[7] Ps. cxxxii. 13
[8] See 2 Sa. v. 6, 7
[9] 2 Sa. vi. 17
[10] Ps. xv. 1
[11] Ps. xxiv. 3

So he sang of God's vindication of His anointed, of God's triumph over Christ's enemies, of God's purpose to set His king upon His holy hill of Zion.[1]

David also foresaw that, when God thus enthroned His Christ, it would be at God's own right hand. Let us quote his words from Psalm cx:

> The Lord said unto my Lord, Sit thou at my right hand, until I make thine enemies thy footstool. The Lord shall send the rod of thy strength out of Zion: rule thou in the midst of thine enemies.[2]

These words indicate that the Zion out of which Christ is to rule is to be in heaven, not in Palestine. And it was in heaven that Christ did thus sit down after His resurrection and ascension. Notice also that in his preaching on the day of Pentecost. Peter claimed that it was by thus exalting Christ to His own right hand in heaven that God fulfilled His oath to David to raise up Christ to sit on David's throne.[3] The fulfilment of God's promise to David is therefore heavenly, not earthly.

It is, therefore, in heaven that the exalted Christ now appears before God, as the Priest of His people as well as their King.[4] Because of this He does what David could not do—gives to those who trust in Him fitness to come boldly into God's presence in free access and joyful fellowship as God's people. By grace we can ascend into the hill of the Lord, and stand in His holy place. This mount Zion, where Jesus reigns as King, and where His people are intended to realize their oneness with God and with one another, is the heavenly, not the earthly Jerusalem. This is, to quote a striking phrase from Isaiah, 'the mount of the congregation',[5] the true meeting-place of the Lord's people.[6] So Christians may sing, not with reference to Palestine, but with reference to their new life in Christ 'in heavenly places',[7]

> I was glad when they said unto me, Let us go into the house of the Lord. Our feet shall stand within thy gates, O Jerusalem. Jerusalem is builded as a city that is compact together: whither

[1] See Ps. ii. 1–8 [2] Ps. cx. 1, 2 [3] See Acts ii. 29–36
[4] See Ps. cx. 4; Zc. vi. 12, 13; Heb. viii. 1, ix. 24
[5] Is. xiv. 13 [6] Cf. Heb. xii. 22–24 [7] See Eph. ii. 4–6

> the tribes go up, the tribes of the Lord, unto the testimony of Israel, to give thanks unto the name of the Lord.[1]

Those who in Old Testament times were inspired prophetically to anticipate the exaltation of God's Christ to God's right hand, and the accompanying establishment of the heavenly Zion as the city where He reigns, also foresaw an accompanying enlargement of the scope of His dominion and of the membership of His city to embrace not just the Jewish race, but men of all nations. So David foresaw that, when God thus set His King upon His holy hill of Zion, He would say unto Him:

> Ask of me, and I shall give thee the heathen for thine inheritance, and the uttermost parts of the earth for thy possession.[2]

Similarly both Isaiah and Micah record the sure prospect of the last days, namely that

> the mountain of the Lord's house shall be established in the top of the mountains, and shall be exalted above the hills; and all nations shall flow unto it. And many people shall go and say, Come ye, and let us go up to the mountain of the Lord, to the house of the God of Jacob; and he will teach us of his ways, and we will walk in his paths: for out of Zion shall go forth the law, and the word of the Lord from Jerusalem.[3]

Or again, through Zechariah, the word of the Lord came:

> Sing and rejoice, O daughter of Zion: for, lo, I come, and I will dwell in the midst of thee, saith the Lord. And many nations shall be joined to the Lord in that day, and shall be my people.[4] Yea, many people and strong nations shall come to seek the Lord of hosts in Jerusalem, and to pray before the Lord.[5]

Zion will thus arise and shine. The glory of the Lord will rise, and be seen, upon her. Then, foretold Isaiah,

> The Gentiles shall come to thy light.[6]
> Thy sons shall come from far.[7]
> And all they that despised thee shall bow themselves down at the soles of thy feet; and they shall call thee, The city of the Lord, The Zion of the Holy One of Israel.[8]

It was our Lord Himself, who implied by His teaching that

[1] Ps. cxxii. 1–4 [2] See Ps. ii. 6–8 [3] Is. ii. 2, 3; cf. Mi. iv. 1, 2
[4] Zc. ii. 10, 11 [5] Zc viii. 22 [6] Is. lx. 3 [7] Is. lx. 4 [8] Is. lx. 14

this prophecy would find fulfilment in the company of His disciples, the citizens of the kingdom of heaven. For it was to them that He said:

> Ye are the light of the world. A city that is set on an hill cannot be hid.[1]

To this city of God the prophets foresaw that citizens would be brought from the ends of the earth, to become sons and daughters both of God and of Zion, and members of the true Israel of God.[2] Indeed, the psalmist was inspired to declare of Zion that God would incorporate members of outside Gentile races, the age-long enemies of God's people, Egypt and Babylon, Philistia and Tyre, and write down their names on the roll as born in Zion. So we read:

> And of Zion it shall be said, This and that man was born in her. . . The Lord shall count, when he writeth up the people, that this man was born there.[3]

Or we find that Isaiah declares:

> In that day shall Israel be the third with Egypt and with Assyria, even a blessing in the midst of the land: whom the Lord of hosts shall bless, saying, Blessed be Egypt my people, and Assyria the work of my hands, and Israel mine inheritance.[4]

Commenting on these words, J. A. Alexander wrote:

'In order to express once more and in the most emphatic manner the admission of Egypt and Assyria to the privileges of the chosen people, he selects three titles commonly bestowed upon the latter exclusively, to wit, *God's people*, *the work of his hands*, and *his inheritance*, and these three he distributes to the three united powers without discrimination or invidious distinction . . . When he . . . describes these representatives of heathenism as received into the covenant, and sharing with the church of God its most distinctive titles, we have one of the clearest and most striking predictions of the calling of the Gentiles that the word of God contains.'[5]

In order to appreciate fully what is made known in the New Testament concerning the character and destiny of God's

[1] Mt. v. 14 [2] See Is. xliii. 1–7 [3] See Ps. lxxxvii. 4–6
[4] Is. xix. 24, 25 [5] *Commentary on Isaiah*, p. 364

people, we need not only to see how it is described in language which takes its rise from the limited earthly story of God's dealings with the Jewish people in Palestine, but also to understand that, in its outworked fulfilment in Christ, it is neither limited, nor earthly, neither exclusively Jewish, nor literally Palestinian, but both universal and heavenly, embracing all races, and exalted to the heavens.

We may sum up this chapter by quoting in full Isaac Watts' well-known hymn:

How pleased and blest was I
To hear the people cry,
'Come let us seek our God today!'
Yes, with a cheerful zeal
We haste to Zion's hill,
And there our vows and homage pay.

Zion, thrice happy place,
Adorned with wondrous grace,
And walls of strength embrace thee round;
In thee our tribes appear,
To pray, and praise, and hear
The sacred gospel's joyful sound.

There David's greater Son
Hath fixed His royal throne;
He sits for grace and judgment there.
He bids the saints be glad,
He makes the sinner sad,
And humble souls rejoice with fear.

May peace attend thy gate,
And joy within thee wait
To bless the soul of every guest.
The man that seeks thy peace,
And wishes thine increase,
A thousand blessings on him rest.

My tongue repeats her vows,
Peace to this sacred house!
For there my friends and kindred dwell.
And since my glorious God
Makes thee His blest abode,
My soul shall ever love thee well.

II. NEW TESTAMENT FULFILMENT

CHAPTER FOUR

IN CHRIST

IN the Old Testament story, over against the haunting awareness of continual human failure, there is frequently set the promise of a coming better day of divine fulfilment. So, for instance, we read:

> Behold, the days come, saith the Lord, that I will make a new covenant with the house of Israel, and with the house of Judah: not according to the covenant that I made with their fathers in the day that I took them by the hand to bring them out of the land of Egypt; which my covenant they brake, although I was an husband unto them, saith the Lord: but this shall be the covenant that I will make with the house of Israel; After those days, saith the Lord, I will put my law in their inward parts, and write it in their hearts; and will be their God, and they shall be my people.[1]

In this connection, it is directly significant that the second part of our Christian Scriptures has come to be called the 'New Testament' or 'Covenant'. For this is its great theme, the fulfilment of God's promises of better things for His chosen people. In its establishment and accomplishment this new covenant of God with men is directly dependent, first, upon the work of God's Son, and, second, upon the work of God's Spirit. It is these personal activities of God Himself which give the Christian gospel its crowning supremacy.

Jesus, we are told, was made 'a surety',[2] or 'mediator of a better covenant, which was established upon better promises'.[3] The covenant was ratified, and the promised blessings assured 'by means of death'—the death of the mediator.[4] So, in the upper room, when He took the cup, and gave it to His disciples, Jesus said:

[1] See Je. xxxi. 31–34 [2] Heb. vii. 22 [3] Heb. viii. 6
[4] See Heb. ix. 15

> Drink ye all of it; for this is my blood of the new testament (or 'covenant'), which is shed for many for the remission of sins.[1]

The complementary quickening and enablement, which are necessary if the redeemed are henceforth to do God's will, is the work of the promised indwelling Spirit. So Ezekiel, foreseeing this better day, had been given to utter this word of the Lord:

> And I will put my spirit within you, and cause you to walk in my statutes, and ye shall keep my judgments, and do them.[2]

Also, the apostle Paul, glorying in his God-given ministry in the gospel of Christ, wrote:

> But our sufficiency is of God; who also hath made us able ministers of the new testament (or 'covenant'); not of the letter, but of the spirit: for the letter killeth, but the spirit giveth life.[3]

For, under the covenant of Sinai, the demands of the law only made condemnation and death certain. By contrast, under the new covenant, the Spirit gives us new life, and endows us with the power for its practical expression in fulfilling the demands of God's righteousness.[4] So, in fulfilment of the promised new covenant, God makes sinful men partakers of salvation and of fullness of life in two complementary ways—in Christ, and by His Spirit. Let us consider each of these in more detail, giving our attention to the former in this chapter, and to the latter in chapter five.

The Old Testament is characteristically forward-looking. In various ways it abounds in promises of One who is to come, who is to fulfil in His Person, and by His work, the destiny of the people of God. So we learn that David is to have a greater Son, the Lord's anointed, i.e. the Messiah or the Christ, whom God will set upon the throne, and to whom the Lord will give the kingdom.[5] Isaiah prophesied of One who, as Jehovah's Servant, would fulfil the destiny of Israel by personally bearing the people's sin. He would then be exalted to enjoy

[1] Mt. xxvi. 27, 28
[2] Ezk. xxxvi. 27
[3] 2 Cor. iii. 5, 6
[4] See Rom. viii. 2–4
[5] See e.g. Ps. ii; Is. ix. 6, 7

the far-reaching consequences of His divinely-ordained humiliation, and to share them with His people.[1] Daniel was given a vision of 'one like the Son of man', who was vindicated at the throne of God in heaven, and given a universal and everlasting kingdom, a kingdom to be possessed by 'the saints of the most High'.[2]

The Gospel records provide evidence that in varying ways, often more implicit than explicit, Jesus claimed to be the Messiah.[3] He indicated even more plainly that He was Jehovah's Servant, destined to suffer to ransom the many.[4] He openly called Himself the Son of man; and even claimed publicly that, as such, He was going to enjoy the prophetically foreshadowed vindication.[5] He referred to Himself as 'the bridegroom',[6] a term used in the Old Testament to describe Jehovah's covenant relation to His people. He also called Himself 'the shepherd' which involved, as He said, direct relation to 'the sheep of the flock'.[7]

During His public ministry Jesus unmistakably acted and taught as One whose calling and purpose it was to establish a new community. To begin with, it is true, He offered Himself to the existing community of God's people. As St. John's Gospel records, He opened His public ministry by going to Jerusalem, at the time of the Passover, to cleanse the temple,[8]—a significant act of self-authentication, if only the Jewish leaders had had eyes to see.[9] When they disowned His claims or asked, without expecting any to be forthcoming, for some supporting sign in proof of them, Jesus answered, somewhat enigmatically, 'Destroy this temple, and in three days I will raise it up.' He thus indicated that their attitude and action could lead only to the judgment of destruction, beyond which He saw hope of a new erection, of which He said He Himself would be the builder. At the end of His ministry, in the same temple courts, He went on to claim that, through the mystery of His being 'lifted up', first to the cross, and then

[1] See Is. lii. 13–liii. 12 [2] Dn. vii. 13–22
[3] See e.g. Mt. xxi. 1–5, 12, 13, 37 [4] See Mk. x. 45; Lk. xxii. 37
[5] Mk. xiv. 62 [6] Mk. ii. 19 [7] Mt. xxvi. 31
[8] See Jn. ii. 13–22 [9] See Mal. iii. 1–5

to the throne, the present prince of this world would be cast out in judgment, and He would draw all men unto Himself,[1] and thus Himself become the centre and the King of a new world-wide community.

With this goal in view, Jesus prepared for it during the whole period of His ministry, by gathering around Himself a circle of disciples,[2] by giving them the new law of the new kingdom,[3] by significantly ordaining twelve[4] to be His constant companions, and thus constituting a new synagogue, and indeed, as it proved, thus providing the beginning of the foundation of a new Israel.

At the second Passover of His ministry,[5] Jesus did not go up to Jerusalem. He virtually staged a feast of His own by feeding the multitude in the wilderness. At that feast there was no earthly city or temple, no sacrificial ritual. He Himself, the living Lord in the midst, was the one meeting-place, and the one source of supply; and He gave not sacrifice to God, but thanks to God and gifts to men. Surely this was an anticipation in figure of the coming feast of His people, which He was going to make it possible for them continually to keep, by being first, and once for all, sacrificed for them.[6] For, as He said, 'the bread of God is he which cometh down from heaven, and giveth life unto the world'.[7] What matters henceforth is not to go to some earthly Jerusalem and to share in the ritual of some earthly shrine, but to come to Christ, and to believe on Him. As Jesus went on to say:

> I am the bread of life: he that cometh to me shall never hunger; and he that believeth on me shall never thirst.[8]

Isaiah had spoken in prophecy of a seed to be born who 'shall inherit the Gentiles, and make the desolate cities to be inhabited'.[9] Our Lord in His discourse, to which we have been referring, quoted from Isaiah's prophecy. He said:

> It is written in the prophets, And they shall be all taught of God.

[1] Jn. xii. 31, 32
[2] Mt. v. 1, 2
[3] Mt. v, vi, vii
[4] Mk. iii. 13–19
[5] See Jn. vi, especially verse 4
[6] See 1 Cor. v. 7
[7] Jn. vi. 33
[8] Jn. vi. 35
[9] See Is. liv. 3

> Every man therefore that hath heard, and hath learned of the Father, cometh unto me.[1]

So the new community is to be gathered, the promised seed brought to the birth, as individuals hear the word of God, enjoy the illumination of the Spirit, and come to the Saviour.

Later, to the small group of His personal followers, Jesus said:

> Fear not, little flock; for it is your Father's good pleasure to give you the kingdom.[2]

And, before His death, sitting at table with them in the upper room, Jesus, speaking as the divinely-appointed King, solemnly made over to them in these words the right to participation in His kingdom:

> I appoint unto you a kingdom, as my Father hath appointed unto me; that ye may eat and drink at my table in my kingdom, and sit on thrones judging the twelve tribes of Israel.[3]

As He faced death, therefore, Jesus knew Himself to be without doubt One who was divinely ordained to be King, One who was about to come into His kingdom, and to reign over what He here called, in Old Testament language, 'the twelve tribes of Israel,' but what He called elsewhere 'my church'.[4] On that occasion, when Simon had confessed concerning Jesus, 'Thou art the Christ', our Lord said to him:

> And I say also unto thee, That thou art Peter, and upon this rock I will build my church; and the gates of hell shall not prevail against it.[5]

This simple, short statement, 'I will build my church,' is enough not only to reveal our Lord's intention to have a Church, but also to make us aware that He is the beginning and the end of the true Church, both her Author and her Owner. He does the building; and the Church which He builds is for Himself.

In the same context from which this statement comes, there is evidence that Jesus regarded two things as essential to the building of His Church. One is the acknowledgement by men of His Person in considered confession and self-committal.

[1] Jn. vi. 45 [2] Lk. xii. 32 [3] Lk. xxii. 29, 30
[4] Mt. xvi. 18 [5] Mt. xvi. 16, 18

The other is the accomplishment of His work, a work involving facing death, and triumphing over it in resurrection. To speak metaphorically, as our Lord Himself did, these two elements are the 'stones' with which His Church is built.

In the first place, by His declaration, 'Thou art Peter',[1] our Lord meant, 'Now you are a "stone"'; which is what Jesus prophetically had earlier said he was to become.[2] Jesus also immediately indicated for what purpose He needed stones—in order to build a Church. By the same statement He also implied that the stones which He would use for building would be disciples, and that individuals would become stones when they did what Simon Peter had done, and in true self-committal confessed Jesus to be the Christ. Peter, therefore, had in his possession the simple and sufficient key of knowledge which would give others entrance, like himself, into the kingdom. Later, in his first Epistle, Peter used this knowledge and expounded this theme. For there he says that those who come to Christ become 'as living stones' to be built into a temple or 'spiritual house' for God's service.[3]

Let us quote our Lord's words to Peter more completely. He said: 'Thou art Peter, and upon this rock I will build my church.'[4] There is reference here not only to Peter himself as a 'stone', but also to a 'rock', as something more substantial than a single stone, which is to provide a basis or foundation for the Church. Here 'rock' can refer to Christ Himself, as thus confessed; for, as St. Paul declares explicitly, He is the one indispensable foundation.[5] Or it may refer to the group of disciples, whose mouthpiece Peter had been, who together, as a compact group of 'stones', formed a 'rock' or solid beginning for the Church, to which other stones could be added.[6] In either case there is further emphasis on the necessity of responsive acknowledgement of Christ's Person by committed believers. Only so can Christ's Church be built.

In the second place, our Lord also said, at the same time, and with reference to His building of His Church, 'And the gates

[1] Mt. xvi. 18
[2] See Jn. i. 42
[3] See 1 Pet. ii. 4, 5, RV
[4] Mt. xvi. 18
[5] See 1 Cor. iii. 11; cf. Is. xxviii. 16
[6] Cf. Eph. ii. 20

of hell (RV, 'Hades', RSV, 'death') shall not prevail against it.'[1] In addition, from that time forth began Jesus openly to predict His own death and resurrection.[2] This indicates, as many other Scriptures confirm, that the new Church could not be built until the power of sin and death had been broken by Christ's own death and resurrection.

In this connection the 'stone' metaphor is also given prominence in Scripture, with reference to Christ Himself. He is 'the stone which the builders refused', who, by God's doing, 'is become the head stone of the corner'.[3] It is Christ, crucified, raised, and highly exalted, to whom men must come, 'as unto a living stone, disallowed indeed of men, but chosen of God', and divinely laid 'in Zion', if they would 'as living stones' be built into Christ's Church.[4] The living, exalted Lord is also to be recognized as Himself being the Builder. By His own act He daily adds to His own Church those who are being saved.[5]

The same two ideas, concerning the acknowledgement of Christ's Person and the accomplishment of Christ's work, as essential to the establishment of His Church, are equally to be discerned in our Lord's use of the 'shepherd' metaphor. He said that His sheep would know His voice and follow Him; and that, by such individual response to His call, and attachment to His Person, the 'one flock' would be constituted around the 'one shepherd'.[6] Also, He indicated that the preservation of the sheep depended upon the willingness of the good Shepherd to give His life for the sheep.[7] Similarly we find later that it is 'the God of peace, that brought again from the dead our Lord Jesus, that great shepherd of the sheep', who can be counted on 'through Jesus Christ', and 'through the blood of the everlasting covenant', to make perfect that which concerns 'the sheep'.[8]

Those who share in the one flock which thus emerges

[1] Mt. xvi. 18 [2] See Mt. xvi. 21, xvii. 22, 23
[3] Ps. cxviii. 22; cf. Acts iv. 11 [4] 1 Pet. ii. 4–6 and RV
[5] See Acts ii. 47 [6] See Jn. x. 1–4, 16 (RV), 27
[7] See Jn. x. 10, 11, 15, 28 [8] Heb. xiii. 20, 21

possess all their individual and corporate privileges because of their common personal relation to Christ. Their new life and experience, their new fellowship with one another, become theirs in Him. Its full enjoyment and expression depend upon the active maintenance of their personal relation to Christ in both dependence and devotion. Their entrance into salvation and their increase or renewal of strength are not gained from the community but by direct personal faith in Christ alone.

This is stressed in our Lord's own teaching, when He says:

> Abide in me, and I in you. As the branch cannot bear fruit of itself, except it abide in the vine; no more can ye, except ye abide in me. I am the vine, ye are the branches.[1]

It is noteworthy that Christ did not say, 'I am the root; the Church is the vine; ye are the branches. Abide in the Church; then you will be vitally related to Me, and share My life.' No: He made it explicitly plain that individual life and fruitfulness, as well as one's place in the fellowship which He thus unites and makes one, depend on direct personal abiding in the personal Christ Himself.

Consequently the phrase 'in Christ', or variants of it, becomes a characteristic distinctive description of Christians. They are 'the saints in Christ Jesus'.[2] God makes every blessing theirs 'in Christ'.[3] Their baptism is a sign and seal of initiation 'into Jesus Christ'.[4] They 'have put on Christ'.[5] Henceforth life in all its aspects is to be lived 'in Christ'. They are to 'walk . . . in him: rooted and built up in him'.[6] Particularly are fellow-Christians to show love, or to render appropriate submission and service, towards one another 'in the Lord'.[7]

When many Christians are thought of together, as all sharing in this common personal relation to Christ, they are sometimes described as constituting one body. So St. Paul writes:

> We, who are many, are one body in Christ.[8]
> Now ye are the body of Christ, and members in particular.[9]

[1] Jn. xv. 4, 5 [2] Phil. i. 1 [3] See Eph. i. 3
[4] See Rom. vi. 3 [5] Gal. iii. 27 [6] Col. ii. 6, 7
[7] Rom. xvi. 2; Eph. vi. 1 [8] Rom. xii. 5, RV [9] 1 Cor. xii. 27

Here, as the metaphor suggests, the different members complement one another. They have a measure of interdependence. They are meant to realize and to enjoy life in Christ together, and in the service of one another. But the place of each member in the body, both his vital connection with it, and his power to function in it in his own particular way, depend on direct personal relation to Christ as the Head. Living function in the body is not entered into just by being connected with the body. Every member must be vitally and personally connected with the Head. This truth is stressed more than once in the Epistles of the New Testament. For instance, St. Paul declares it to be God's purpose for us

> that we . . . speaking the truth in love, may grow up into him in all things, which is the head, even Christ: from whom the whole body fitly joined together and compacted by that which every joint supplieth, according to the effectual working in the measure of every part, maketh increase of the body unto the edifying of itself in love.[1]

Here what is emphasized is that the whole body will be fitly joined together only as every joint or part, by enablement direct from Christ, the Head, fulfils its own particular function. Similarly, in writing to the Colossians, St. Paul warns Christians of the danger of being beguiled through

> not holding the Head, from which all the body by joints and bands having nourishment ministered, and knit together, increaseth with the increase of God.[2]

Again, the emphasis is on the necessity of every part of the body maintaining direct contact with Christ, and drawing its nourishment from Him, in order fully to share in the fellowship and the increase of the whole.

This emphasis is important because some give unhealthy prominence to the Church, and to certain special ministers and ordinances in the Church. They virtually teach that relationship to Christ, and the reception of life and grace from Him, are to be enjoyed through being joined to the Church, and through depending on these other members of the body

[1] Eph. iv. 14–16 [2] Col. ii. 18, 19

whose special ministry it is to mediate Christ and His grace to the body as a whole. The dangers of such teaching being accepted, with all its consequent errors in thought and practice, is increased, and made almost inevitable, if the 'body' phraseology about the Church is interpreted literally, and then applied generally, instead of being—as it plainly should be—interpreted metaphorically, and then applied only within the limits of the particular use and explicit qualification of the metaphor made in the relevant scriptural passages. For, important as fulfilling his place in the larger fellowship of the whole body is, both for every member and for the Church as a whole, it is also important to remember that Christ has promised to be personally accessible and to give Himself to seeking souls both one by one, and in twos or threes.

Let us quote, in conclusion, words which He Himself said:

> If a man love me, he will keep my words: and my Father will love him, and we will come unto him, and make our abode with him.[1]
>
> For where two or three are gathered together in my name, there am I in the midst of them.[2]

[1] Jn. xiv. 23; cf. Mt. xi. 27–29; Jn. vi. 35
[2] Mt. xviii. 20

CHAPTER FIVE

BY THE SPIRIT: THROUGH FAITH

THE Person and work of Jesus Christ the incarnate Son of God are, as we have seen, fundamental to the Christian gospel and to the establishment of the Christian Church. What the Son of God came into the world to make possible by His death and resurrection as God's Christ is now, by His gift, made actual in the experience of men, by the work of God the Spirit, when they believe in Him. Fulfilment of God's purposes 'in Christ' is, therefore, wrought out and made ours 'by the Spirit' and 'through faith'. These two activities, the work of the divine Spirit and the response of human faith, are essential to the emergence of the saved community. St Paul declared that:

> Christ hath redeemed us . . . that the blessing of Abraham might come on the Gentiles through Jesus Christ; that we might receive the promise of the Spirit through faith.[1]

This, he tells us, is how God's promise to Abraham, that members of all races of the earth should through him share in blessing from God,[2] is to be fulfilled. Note the three essentials. They are (a) 'through Jesus Christ'; (b) by men receiving 'the promise of the Spirit'; and (c) 'through faith'. In the previous chapter we considered the first of these, namely that all fulfilment is 'in Christ'. In this chapter we are to consider the other two; that all fulfilment is 'by the Spirit', and 'through faith'.

THE WORK OF THE SPIRIT

The Spirit of God is the Executor of the Godhead. The will of the Father and the word of the Son find completion and fulfilment in the work of the Spirit. God acts, 'not by might,

[1] Gal. iii. 13, 14 [2] See Gn. xviii. 18, xxii. 18

nor by power, but by my spirit, saith the Lord of hosts.'[1] For instance, when Abraham and Sarah were childless, God worked to give them a son. As we have already seen, it was through special, supernatural, divine intervention that Isaac was born. Isaac's birth is set in Scripture in radical contrast to the birth of Ishmael. For Ishmael was born, without difficulty, in the natural way, of Abraham and Hagar. In the New Testament the full significance of this difference is emphasized and interpreted by the declaration that Ishmael was 'born after the flesh', and Isaac was born 'after the Spirit'.[2] In familiar words our Lord made the same distinction when He talked to Nicodemus:

> That which is born of the flesh is flesh; and that which is born of the Spirit is spirit. Marvel not that I said unto thee, Ye must be born again.[3]

No-one, therefore, can enter the new community, and belong to the kingdom of God, by natural birth. Entrance is possible only to those who are born again of God's Spirit.[4] This is 'the blessing of Abraham', which Christ came to make possible for men, the blessing of being born again of God's Spirit and enjoying eternal life. Indeed, when Nicodemus asked, 'How can these things be?' this is the answer which Jesus Himself gave:

> As Moses lifted up the serpent in the wilderness, even so must the Son of man be lifted up: that whosoever believeth in him should not perish, but have eternal life.[5]

This ability to baptize men with God's Spirit and to quicken them to new life is the distinctive mark and the exclusive prerogative of God's Christ. John the Baptist foretold this, when he said:

> I indeed baptize you with water; but one mightier than I cometh . . . he shall baptize you with the Holy Ghost.[6]

Peter also, on the day of Pentecost, explained the transformed condition of the disciples, as being due to the outpouring of the Spirit by Jesus Christ, now alive and exalted.

[1] Zc. iv. 6 [2] Gal. iv. 29 [3] Jn. iii. 6, 7
[4] See Jn. iii. 3–5 [5] Jn. iii. 9, 14, 15 [6] Lk. iii. 16

> This Jesus hath God raised up . . . Therefore being by the right hand of God exalted, and having received of the Father the promise of the Holy Ghost, he hath shed forth this, which ye now see and hear.[1]

This outpouring of the Spirit provided practical proof that the day of fulfilment had come, and that Jesus was indeed made by God 'both Lord and Christ'.[2] This outpouring of the Spirit also bound all who shared in it into a vital fellowship. The day of Pentecost has been rightly called the birthday of the Church. For on that day the disciples of Jesus were not only individually given new life from above; they were also given it together by the one Spirit, and were thereby united as one family. The offer of personal participation in this same gift from the exalted Lord immediately became an essential part of the gospel which was preached. Peter explicitly declared on the same day of Pentecost that all who acknowledged Jesus as Lord, and received baptism in His name as a pledge or seal, would enjoy the two fundamental benefits of which water-baptism symbolically speaks, the blessing of cleansing from sin through Christ's death, and the blessing of new life by the quickening gift and indwelling of the divine Spirit.[3]

The consequent privilege and mark of the true Christian community or Church of Christ is, therefore, the *koinōnia* (to use the Greek word) or fellow-sharing of the Spirit.[4] Such possession of the indwelling Spirit of God by every individual is likewise the decisive mark and seal of every man's participation in Christ, and of his membership in the community of His people. For, on the one hand, 'no man can say that Jesus is the Lord, but by the Holy Ghost';[5] and, on the other hand, 'if any man have not the Spirit of Christ, he is none of his'.[6] It is, too, this same Spirit who not only brings new life, but also guarantees to all to whom He is given, endurance to the end, and ultimate participation in the full inheritance.[7]

Before His death our Lord prayed to the Father that His

[1] Acts ii. 32, 33 [2] See Acts ii. 16, 17, 36 [3] See Acts ii. 38
[4] See Phil. ii. 1; 2 Cor. xiii. 14 [5] 1 Cor. xii. 3
[6] Rom. viii. 9 [7] See 2 Cor. i. 21, 22; Eph. i. 13, 14; Phil. i. 6

followers might be made one as He and the Father were one in the Godhead, that is, in the unity of the Spirit.[1] This prayer was answered when, as the exalted Christ triumphant over sin and death, Jesus received from the Father the promised Spirit and gave Him to His disciples.[2] The distinctive unity of Christians is, therefore, divinely created. Christ Himself makes His people one in the unity of the Spirit. St. Paul puts it thus:

> For by one Spirit are we all baptized into one body, whether we be Jews or Gentiles, whether we be bond or free.[3]

So, on the day of Pentecost, by this baptism or outpouring of the Spirit on the company of disciples, the one Church of Christ emerged or was born. This Church was, and still is, one in both senses of the word; that is, it is both united and unique. For there is only one Spirit of God; and He unites in one the company of those to whom He is thus uniquely given by the glorified Christ.

Another way in which this truth has sometimes been expressed is to speak of the Church of Christ as the 'Spirit-bearing body' or, to quote St. Paul's words, as 'an habitation of God through the Spirit'.[4] Here it is important to recognize clearly how new members are added to the Church. Although the Church possesses the Spirit, she cannot give the Spirit who possesses her to those outside her number, and therefore cannot, by joining them to herself, join them to Christ. Such a view, virtually held by some, is excessively ecclesiastical rather than truly Christian. It gives to the Church a place and a ministry which belongs to Christ alone. The truth is that only the exalted Lord can baptize outsiders with the one Spirit; and it is by so doing, when they acknowledge Him as Lord, and call upon His name, or when they repent and are baptized in His name, that He adds them to His Church. So we read concerning the early days of the Church that 'the Lord added to the church daily such as should be saved', or 'those that were being saved'.[5]

In the light of these truths it is important to recognize that,

[1] See Jn. xvii. 20–23 [2] See Acts ii. 33; cf. Jn. xv. 26
[3] 1 Cor. xii. 13 [4] Eph. ii. 22 [5] Acts ii. 47 and RV

in the New Testament, Christians are not exhorted to create a unity among themselves, as though none existed. Rather they are told to give diligence first to preserve, and then to give full and mature expression to, the Spirit-given unity which God has created.[1] Such unity, by its very nature, is fostered and consummated as fellow-believers in Christ enjoy and express together their fellowship with the one Lord in the one Spirit. It is not dependent on, and need not interminably await, the organizational integration or harmonization of the institutional framework of man-made denominations.

We find, too, that in the early days of the Church the decisive evidence that individuals belonged to the new community and were to be welcomed as brethren in Christ was their possession of the one Spirit. On the one hand, concern was aroused if any seemed to lack this. Prayer might be offered with laying on of hands for sensible manifestation of the Spirit's presence, or teaching given in order to lead them to decisive faith in Jesus as the Christ and to baptism in His name, so that He might then give them of His Spirit.[2] On the other hand, when there was undeniable evidence of the Spirit's presence, conviction that God had accepted men as members of His people was created. At times, indeed, it was compelled, in the face of natural prejudice and preference, to think otherwise. So Cornelius and his household were accepted as belonging to the new community, and baptized without further demand being made of them, because, as Peter put it when interrogated concerning his behaviour,

> God gave them the like gift as he did unto us, who believed on the Lord Jesus Christ; what was I, that I could withstand God?[3]

Similarly, when Barnabas was sent by the church in Jerusalem to investigate what was happening in the independent and somewhat revolutionary group in Antioch, he was persuaded by the manifest work of the Spirit of God in their midst that they must be treated without reserve as full brethren in Christ.[4] This is still a proper, decisive criterion. Where the

[1] See Eph. iv. 3, 11–16
[2] See Acts viii. 14–17, xix. 1–6
[3] Acts xi. 17
[4] See Acts xi. 19–24

fruits of the Spirit's presence appear in men's individual lives and in their corporate activity, including the full confession of Jesus as Lord, their living membership in Christ and in His one Church ought to be fully acknowledged. For, as some have rightly expressed it, 'Where the Spirit is, there the Church is.'

JUSTIFICATION BY FAITH ONLY

The complementary truth next to be considered is that, on man's side, the promised blessing from God which is made ours 'in Christ' and 'by the Spirit' is to be possessed and enjoyed 'through faith'. Men and women enter the company of the redeemed and the sanctified as, one by one, in response to the invitation of the gospel, they come to Christ as their personal Lord and Saviour, in confession and renunciation of wrong-doing, and in the confidence, committal and obedience of faith.

Christ Himself, 'the man Christ Jesus', the personal, living, exalted Lord, is for them the one all-sufficient 'mediator between God and men'.[1] Other Christians, particularly ministers of the gospel, and the local congregational worship, particularly the sacraments of the gospel, may commonly also be active in connection with such response to Christ. But at the decisive point of entrance into God's kingdom they have no absolutely indispensable place. Their witness may be needed and used, it is true, to show the outsider the way, to bring him to the threshold, to assure him of the benefits to be found within. But Christ alone is the door by which every individual must enter.[2] It is He alone who 'quickeneth whom he will'.[3] None but He can say, as He solemnly asserted:

> Verily, verily, I say unto you, He that heareth my word, and believeth on him that sent me, hath everlasting life, and shall not come into condemnation; but is passed from death unto life.[4]

The repentant sinner who thus trusts in the Saviour is justified before God by faith only, in Christ alone. This gives

[1] 1 Tim. ii. 5 [2] See Jn. x. 7–10 [3] See Jn. v. 21
[4] Jn. v. 24

him, as St. Paul explicitly declares, peace with God, free access by grace to God's presence whenever he desires to draw near, and the sure hope of a share in the coming glorification of Christ's Church. It also means that he is at once given the Holy Spirit.[1] There are many Scriptures which confirm this.[2] Over against the pretentious claims made by some for the Church, the priest, and the sacraments, there is no truth that is more fundamental than this to the gospel of Christ and to truly biblical faith.

It is particularly noteworthy that Peter in his first Epistle unmistakably indicates that this is how the true Church emerges, through the active expression by men of simple personal faith in the personal Lord. He thinks of his readers as individually coming to the living exalted Christ. He describes Him in scriptural metaphor as the divinely-chosen corner-stone, set in place in Zion; and so thinks of his readers as 'living stones', coming to be joined to the 'living stone'. He then adds:

> And he that believeth on him shall not be put to shame. For you therefore which believe is the preciousness.[3]

In these verses the whole stress is on personal coming to Christ, and on faith, on faith alone, on believing in the personal Lord. It can be said of all who make this decisive response to Christ, and who are thus built by Him into the Church which He is building,

> Ye are an elect race, a royal priesthood, a holy nation, a people for God's own possession.[4]

In his Epistle to the Galatians St. Paul wrote, 'For we through the Spirit wait for the hope of righteousness by faith'.[5] Commenting on this. James Denney wrote: 'The Spirit and faith are correlative terms, and each of them covers, from a different point of view, all that is meant by Christianity. Regarded from the side of God and His grace and power in initiating and maintaining it, Christianity is the Spirit; regarded from the side of man and his action and responsibility in relation to

[1] See Rom. v. 1, 2, 5 [2] E.g. cf. Eph. i. 13, 14; Gal. iii. 2
[3] 1 Pet. ii. 6, 7, RV [4] 1 Pet. ii. 9, RV [5] Gal. v. 5

God, it is faith.'[1] Similarly, the plain implication of what St. Paul wrote earlier in the same Epistle is that his readers became Christians when they 'received the Spirit', and that they received the Spirit 'by the hearing of faith'.[2]

What is noteworthy is that, at this point in the apostle's statements, there is no mention of the necessity for receiving water baptism or for the laying on of hands before the gift of the Spirit and the consequent vital membership in the one true Church can be enjoyed. The one indispensable and sufficient essential is faith. Later in the same Epistle, Paul confirms this distinctive emphasis again when he asserts that in Christ Jesus what avails is not outward ceremonies, like circumcision or baptism, but, on the one hand, 'a new creature',[3] the work of the quickening Spirit, and, on the other hand, 'faith working through love'.[4]

Similarly, because of his experience in the house of Cornelius, St. Peter contended at the council of Jerusalem that personal, responsive faith in Christ and the divine gift of the quickening Spirit are decisive in determining full membership in the Church of Christ; and that nothing else is to be laid upon any as necessary to salvation and to fellowship in Christ.[5]

It is such plain and reiterated scriptural and apostolic testimony that accounts for the historic evangelical and reformed emphasis on justification by faith only. So we believe that, if an unbaptized unbeliever heard the gospel preached, came to Christ in personal repentance and faith, and then subsequently was quite rightly baptized, that he would receive the Spirit from the Lord in new birth and become a living member of the one true Church when he believed in Christ, and not later at his baptism. The baptism, rightly entered into, would give the spiritual essentials (responsive faith and the gift of the quickening Spirit) solemn and visible confirmation, and would openly mark its recipient as a member of Christ's visible congregation. Or, should baptism have been administered before the individual concerned thus makes actual,

[1] *Dictionary of Christ and the Gospels*, Vol. I, p. 738
[2] See Gal. iii. 2 [3] Gal. vi. 15, RV [4] Gal. v. 6, RV
[5] See Acts xv. 7–11

personal response to Christ in saving faith, such a baptism may be understood as a seal upon God's promises, a seal given in His name in pledge of what He does for all who are in Christ. But it is the subsequent response to Christ of personal faith and the incoming, by Christ's gift, of the divine Spirit that are the occasion when such a man becomes a living member of Christ, rather than the day of his participation in the ceremony of baptism without these accompanying essentials. We can sum up the last two chapters by saying, that God makes us His people in Christ, by the Spirit, through faith.

CHAPTER SIX

THE OLD AND THE NEW ISRAEL

AS we have already recognized in chapter three, the God-given revelation which the Old Testament Scriptures contain provides prophetic anticipations of a large fulfilment. We have in the Old Testament what are described in the New Testament as 'figures of the true'[1] and 'a shadow of good things to come'.[2] Such figures are of value, because they serve to disclose the existence, and in measure to describe the character, of corresponding realities. Before sending forth His Son in 'the fulness of the time',[3] God prepared men's minds to appreciate the certainty and the content of His purposes for mankind by special typical dealings with a small selected earthly nation. His treatment during this Old Testament period of a chosen race as His special people, and their connection, by His providential ordering, with a promised land and a holy city, are all figurative of the ultimate truth and correspond to the divinely predestined, heavenly realities, namely God's choosing of an elect people in Christ, and their possession of an eternal inheritance in the heavenlies, in the heavenly Jerusalem or true city of God.

In the Old Testament, therefore, there is anticipatory figure. The details, while literally true in their original earthly and historical context, are often ultimately of chief significance figuratively. They typify or foreshadow the larger purposes of God for men in Christ. The New Testament records this outworked fulfilment. It reveals the truth itself, the good things that were to come. Here the fulfilment, just because it is ultimately spiritual and heavenly, unseen and eternal, can often be appreciated only when it is interpreted or described to us by the aid of the preparatory Old Testament figures,

[1] Heb. ix. 24 [2] Heb. x. 1 [3] See Gal. iv. 4

which are understandable just because they were earthly and historical. So we are meant, in our use of the Scriptures, to move by the aid of their figurative use from the earthly to an appreciation of a higher realm of spiritual reality where the true fulfilment is found. The things seen are thus recognized as fleeting shadows of things unseen. The things unseen are the spiritual and eternal realities.

In concrete illustration of this figurative use of natural objects we may notice how our Lord, having talked to the woman of Samaria about the actual physical water from Jacob's well, went on to say:

> Whosover drinketh of this water shall thirst again: but whosoever drinketh of the water that I shall give him shall never thirst; but the water that I shall give him shall be in him a well of water springing up into everlasting life.[1]

Thus, starting from the earthly and the natural, Jesus used the reference to water to speak to the woman of the higher, unseen, spiritual reality, the indwelling Spirit. In the same way we believe that reference to Israel and to Zion occur in the Scriptures, first in reference to an earthly race and place, but ultimately in reference to the spiritual community and the heavenly city of God's eternal purpose.

Here there is a danger which the history of the Jewish people itself tragically illustrates. Some have become so attached to the figure (rightly convinced that it is divinely ordained) that, when its fulfilment is offered to them, they refuse to let the figure be superseded by the fulfilment. They therefore reject the fulfilment in order still to hold fast to the figure. This is how many of the Jews acted at the time of our Lord. They rejected Christ in order still to hold fast to their earthly temple and their ceremonial law. What adds to the irony of their folly is that the things to which they sought to adhere were values which could no longer be preserved. For, having served their purpose as figures of the true, they were destined under God's providence to pass away, now that fulfilment had come in Christ.[2]

[1] Jn. iv. 13, 14
[2] See Lk. v. 36–39; Mt. xxiii. 38, xxiv. 1, 2; Heb. viii. 13

Now the distinctive mark of God's own fulfilment of His purposes in Christ is 'new creation'.

> Wherefore if any man is in Christ, he is a new creature (mg., 'there is a new creation'): the old things are passed away; behold, they are become new.[1]

The old man, the sinful nature, must come under judgment, and be crucified with Christ, in order that the new man may be raised up in Him. This principle found its inevitable application in the history of the chosen community, the Israel of God. For the Jewish race, although a figure of the true, was only the natural seed of Abraham, and therefore sinful, prone to failure and rebellion, bound to come under divine judgment. The very appearance and activity among them of God's Christ made this failure and rebellion decisively manifest. They rejected Him. This, as our Lord plainly and solemnly indicated, made divine judgment inevitable and imminent. So Jesus foretold the destruction of temple, city and nation. The Jews were to lose their place of privilege. But God's purposes were not to fail. A new Israel would be raised up, a spiritual seed, to whom their privilege would be given, and who, by the grace of God, would not fail as the natural Israel had done. So, said Jesus,

> The kingdom of God shall be taken from you, and given to a nation bringing forth the fruits thereof.[2]

The mystery and miracle of resurrection from the dead, which lies at the heart of the gospel of Christ, paradoxically combines the two ideas of new creation and of real continuity with what existed before. This is true of the resurrection of the body. It is equally true in principle of the resurrection of the Israel of God. When Christ died the order of things under the old Israel ceased to be, and their inevitable dissolution followed. When Christ was raised from the dead a new Israel was begun in Him.

Help to a fuller understanding of this truth may be gained from some of the figurative language of the Bible. Let us

[1] 2 Cor. v. 17, RV

[2] Mt. xxi. 43

consider first what the Scriptures have to say concerning the vine or the vineyard of God. In Psalm lxxx we read:

> Thou hast brought a vine out of Egypt: thou hast cast out the heathen, and planted it. Thou preparedst room before it, and didst cause it to take deep root, and it filled the land.[1]

In Isaiah v, following 'a song of my beloved touching his vineyard', the prophet states:

> For the vineyard of the Lord of hosts is the house of Israel, and the men of Judah his pleasant plant.[2]

Later, we find that our Lord Himself told a parable about a vineyard and about wicked husbandmen, who ill-treated the servants of the lord of the vineyard, and finally killed his son, and cast him out of the vineyard.

> What shall therefore the lord of the vineyard do? he will come and destroy the husbandmen, and will give the vineyard unto others.[3]

Here plainly is judgment on the old Israel. Lest there should be any doubt, let us note that the evangelist records, 'they knew that he had spoken the parable against them'.[4]

Yet that is not the end of the vine of God. For not long after telling this parable, and immediately before His death, Jesus said:

> I am the true vine. . . . I am the vine, ye are the branches: He that abideth in me, and I in him, the same bringeth forth much fruit.[5]

Clearly then the depiction of the people of Israel in Old Testament times as 'a vine' was a figure of the true. 'The true vine' is Christ. The new and true Israel is constituted in Him. The true Israelites are not the Jewish Israelites (nor the British Israelites), who claim to be physically descended from Abraham, but the Christo-Israelites, whose one ground of belonging to Israel is that they belong to Christ. So St. Paul wrote:

> And if ye be Christ's, then are ye Abraham's seed, and heirs according to the promise.[6]

[1] Ps. lxxx. 8, 9 [2] Is. v. 1–7 [3] Mk. xii. 9
[4] Mk. xii. 12 [5] Jn. xv. 1, 5 [6] Gal. iii. 29

Let us also consider what the Scriptures have to say about the house or temple of God. By rejecting Christ's claim to be its Lord, the Jews brought destruction upon their temple. Jesus disowned it as His. It was left unto them desolate; and its destruction foretold.[1] But Jesus also said that He would raise up a new temple.[2] Similarly, after foretelling the judgment which must fall on the wicked husbandmen Jesus went on to say:

> And have ye not read this scripture; The stone which the builders rejected is become the head of the corner . . . ?[3]

This clearly was a reference to Himself as the sole connecting link between the old Israel and the new, and as the focal centre of a new community, which, as a house of living stones, was to constitute the true house of God, of which the temple of stone in the earthly Jerusalem was but a passing figure.

The New Testament Scriptures also provide evidence that the implications of such statements of our Lord were fully understood and explicitly taught in the early Church. For we find in the Epistles that descriptions reserved in the Old Testament for the one chosen Jewish race are transferred and directly applied to the new Christian community which was constituted, not by descent from Abraham, nor by circumcision and the observance of the ceremonial law, but by acknowledgement of Christ as Lord and by personal faith in Him. So, for instance, St. Peter takes phrases used of the old Israel in the book of Exodus and elsewhere, and applies them to his Christian readers, most of them not Jews at all but Gentiles. He says:

> But ye are an elect race, a royal priesthood, a holy nation, a people for God's own possession, that ye may shew forth the excellencies of him who called you out of darkness into his marvellous light.[4]

In its context, this quotation specifically brings before us the additional important truth that the new Israel knows no

[1] See Mt. xxiii. 38, xxiv. 1, 2 [2] Jn. ii. 19 [3] Mk. xii. 10

[4] 1 Pet. ii. 9, RV; cf. Ex. xix. 5, 6; Dt. vii. 6; Is. xliii. 20, 21; Gal. vi. 16; Tit. ii. 14; Rev. v. 9, 10

racial barriers. Membership in it is open in Christ to men of all nations. Not only so; the New Testament documents record repeatedly in this very connection that, while the Jewish people, to whom Christ was particularly promised and to whom He personally came, were slow and largely unwilling to receive Him, Gentiles were quick to embrace the least opportunity to exercise faith and to find hope in Him.

Nor did our Lord Himself resent this, or refuse to welcome such would-be believers. Rather, when a Roman centurion said, 'speak the word only, and my servant shall be healed', Jesus marvelled and said:

> Verily I say unto you, I have not found so great faith, no, not in Israel. And I say unto you, That many shall come from the east and west, and shall sit down with Abraham, and Isaac, and Jacob, in the kingdom of heaven. But the children of the kingdom shall be cast out into outer darkness.[1]

Here our Lord was repeating ideas expressed by the prophet Zechariah.

> Thus saith the Lord of hosts; Behold, I will save my people from the east country, and from the west country; and I will bring them, and they shall dwell in the midst of Jerusalem: and they shall be my people, and I will be their God, in truth and in righteousness.[2]

Let us note that our Lord did not restrict the fulfilment of this prophecy to members of the Jewish race coming to the earthly Jerusalem. Rather He interpreted it in terms of men of all races coming into the one heavenly kingdom, and added that members of the Jewish race who were nominally 'sons of the kingdom' would be cast out.

In the last week before His death, when our Lord cleansed the outer court of the temple, He significantly quoted these words from the prophet Isaiah, 'Is it not written, My house shall be called of all nations the house of prayer?'[3] This had particular relevance because the money-changing and the buying and selling were carried on in the court of the Gentiles.

[1] See Mt. viii. 5–13
[2] Zc. viii. 7, 8
[3] Mk. xi. 17; from Is. lvi. 7

Gentiles were thus prevented from using it as a place of prayer.

It is humanly possible that the reason why some Greeks, who had come up to Jerusalem for the Passover, asked at this time to see Jesus,[1] was because His action had made them aware that He was personally interested in helping them to draw nigh to God. Further, in answer to their request, what Jesus did was to declare:

> The hour is come, that the Son of man should be glorified.
> And I, if I be lifted up from the earth, will draw all men unto me.[2]

Here is the same interest surprisingly developed. Jesus is concerned to make it possible for men of all nations to see Him, and to make Himself the rallying-point for them to unite in thus drawing near to God in and through Him.

Such a fulfilment could take place only if existing barriers separating men from God, and separating Jews from Gentiles, were all broken down. This, as St. Paul later expounds,[3] is exactly what Christ's death achieved. By His death He both reconciled men to God and re-united divided sections of humanity. The old order of the old Israel was completely superseded. The inner veil of the temple was rent in twain, and the outer wall of partition keeping Gentiles outside the commonwealth of Israel was broken down. Those who formerly were far off and without a God to call their own are now made nigh by the blood of Christ. So in the new and the true Israel, fulfilled in Christ, Gentile outsiders become 'fellow heirs' and 'fellow citizens with the saints' and fellow-members 'of the household of God'.

There is, therefore, in the new Israel equal place for Jew and Gentile. Indeed, in Christ, there is no natural distinction between men which allows some in and shuts others out, or gives some priority over others.

> For ye are all the children of God by faith in Christ Jesus. . . . There is neither Jew nor Greek, there is neither bond nor free, there is neither male or female: for ye are all one in Christ Jesus.[4]

[1] See Jn. xii. 20, 21
[2] Jn. xii. 23. 32
[3] See Eph. ii. 11–22
[4] Gal. iii. 26, 28; cf. Col. iii. 10, 11

Finally, while the new Israel is, therefore, a new and very different creation from the old Israel, while the true is intended to surpass and to supersede the figure, there is also a real continuity between the old and the new. There is fundamentally only one 'Israel of God'.[1] So, when our Lord predicted that Gentiles would 'come from the east and west', from outside what He Himself called 'Israel', He also said that they would sit down with ' Abraham, and Isaac, and Jacob, in the kingdom of heaven'.[2] For the true Israelites of Old Testament times belong to the one Israel of God, just as surely as do present-day believers in Christ.

This truth of single continuity is expressed by St. Paul in terms of an olive tree, of which the original branches were Jewish. When these largely failed and were fruitless, they were broken off in judgment, and wild olive branches from outside were grafted in to complete the continuing tree of God. But the divine mercy which makes it possible for unworthy outsiders to be brought in, equally makes it possible for Jews who have been cast out because of their unbelief to be reinstated, if only they will come, as Gentile outsiders come, to acknowledge Christ, and to believe in Him. Indeed, argues St. Paul, is it not more likely that such branches should be able to be grafted back into what was originally 'their own olive tree'?[3]

So the hope of the future for the Jewish people, as well as for the Gentile nations, is Christ. He is the one and only 'hope of Israel'.[4] Men of all races—'of all nations, and kindreds, and people, and tongues'[5]—can and will find a place in the one true Israel of God, through simple, common faith in the one Saviour, 'the Lamb that was slain, which is in the midst of the throne'.[6] What is more, not until the full complement of Jews are added to the full number of elect Gentiles will 'all Israel'[7] be saved, and the end come.

This crowning emphasis of the Scriptures on one final, heavenly and spiritual fulfilment in Christ for Jews as well

[1] Gal. vi. 16
[2] Mt. viii. 10, 11
[3] See Rom. xi. 17–32
[4] Acts xxviii. 20
[5] Rev. vii. 9
[6] Rev. v. 12, vii. 17
[7] Rom. xi. 26

as Gentiles, is confirmed negatively in the New Testament (particularly in the book of Revelation with its abundance of Old Testament phraseology and reference) by the striking fact that it nowhere promises an earthly, national future either for the Jewish race or for Palestine and Jerusalem. Its whole hope and sure promise of fulfilment are concentrated on the spiritual Israel and the heavenly Jerusalem. For the former were but the temporary figure; the latter are the eternally true.

CHAPTER SEVEN

THE ONE TRUE CHURCH

GOD Himself has chosen in Christ from before the foundation of the world to have a people who are to be peculiarly His own and who are to 'be holy and without blame before him in love'.[1] So, in the first place, the one true Church is the Church of God's eternal purpose. All who belong to it are 'elect according to the foreknowledge of God the Father'.[2] They are those whom 'he also did predestinate to be conformed to the image of his Son, that he might be the firstborn among many brethren'.[3]

In the second place, this true Church is the community upon which the eternal Son of God has set His love, and for which, as Man, He gave Himself, to purchase it to Himself and to God, to sanctify and cleanse it, by His blood shed in atoning and redeeming sacrifice.[4] That is why He became Man. He came fully into the sphere where the people of His choice were in bondage and, as Moses had typically done for the Israelites in Egypt, accomplished an 'exodus'[5] in order to bring them out to be God's very own.

When Christ set Himself to redeem and to possess His people, the enemies which stood in the way were sin and its penalty, death. So He faced the necessity of dying for sin, in order that 'the gates of Hades' (or 'the powers of death') might not prevail against, and so prevent, the building of His Church.[6] It is because, as 'the captain of their salvation', He was made 'perfect through sufferings', by tasting death 'for every man', that He can bring the 'many' as 'sons unto glory', and acknowledge them as His 'brethren', the true Church.[7]

[1] See Eph. i. 3–6 [2] 1 Pet. i. 1, 2 [3] Rom. viii. 29
[4] See Eph. v. 25–27; Acts xx. 28; Tit. ii. 14
[5] See Lk. ix. 31, Gk. [6] See Mt. xvi. 18, 21, RV and RSV
[7] See Heb. ii. 9–15

Consequently there emerges the new community of Christ's Church which begins in Christ risen from the dead. When He arose from the dead it was as *the beginning* of the Church. For as 'the firstborn from the dead', He was destined and exalted by God to be 'the head of the body, the church', and 'the firstborn among many brethren'.[1] When 'the God of peace' brought Him up from the dead as 'our Lord Jesus, that great shepherd of the sheep',[2] this was the pledge that all His flock would be raised too, to be united with Him in glory. His elevation by God from the grave to the throne of the universe, there to be given by God to be 'the head over all things to the church, which is his body',[3] explains why (to change the metaphor), in the new building of the Church, Christ as the Stone to which all must be joined, is often referred to as the exalted 'chief corner stone'[4] set on high, rather than as the foundation stone.

The fact, too, that all, who are to become members of this Church, have to be personally related to Christ risen from the dead, and by the gift of His Spirit to share in His risen life, means that the Church thus being built does not really belong to this world, or exist in this present natural order of creation. Rather, because it only emerges on the far side of Christ's death and resurrection, it belongs to 'the world to come',[5] and exists only 'in heavenly places in Christ'.[6]

This truth is manifested in Christian baptism. For our baptism into Christ signifies, on the one hand, the end of our old sinful nature, which is crucified with Him, and on the other, the putting on in Him, through His resurrection, of a new spiritual nature,

> that like as Christ was raised up from the dead by the glory of the Father, even so we also should walk in newness of life.[7]

St. Paul goes even further, and says that we are intended to 'reign in life by . . . Jesus Christ'.[8] Elsewhere he expresses it thus:

> Ye are complete in him, which is the head of all principality and power.[9]

[1] Rom. viii. 29
[2] See Heb. xiii. 20
[3] Eph. i. 22, 23
[4] Eph. ii. 20, 21
[5] Heb. ii. 5
[6] Eph. i. 3, ii. 6
[7] Rom. vi. 3, 4
[8] Rom. v. 17
[9] Col. ii. 10

> But God, who is rich in mercy, for his great love wherewith he loved us, even when we were dead in sins, hath quickened us together with Christ, (by grace ye are saved;) and hath raised us up together, and made us sit together in heavenly places in Christ Jesus.[1]

So Christians are to think of themselves as joined to the chief corner-stone in the heavenly Zion, and as thus finding their place in the temple where God is worshipped. Christians are to think of themselves as reigning with the exalted Lord, who sits as King at God's right hand. Nor is it hard to see in all this a true, heavenly fulfilment of the prophetic utterance of Zechariah:

> Thus speaketh the Lord of hosts, saying, Behold the man whose name is The BRANCH; . . . he shall build the temple of the Lord: . . . and he shall bear the glory, and shall sit and rule upon his throne.[2]

These great truths about the enthroned Christ, and about the Church which is joined to Him on high 'in heavenly places', are not truths which can be discerned by the world, or even seen by Christians' natural eyes. Christians are exhorted, in consequence, to realize these truths by faith, and to adjust themselves and all their actions to them, by thinking, and acting in their light.[3] For Christians are scarcely likely to walk worthily of their heavenly calling if they are influenced solely by what they can see of the visible Church on earth. In this matter of the one true heavenly Church, to which in Christ, and by God's grace, they belong, they are intended rather to be inspired by what cannot be seen. To assert, therefore, as some do, that there is no Church except the visible Church, is to rob Christians of essential truth, of larger vision, and of indispensable inspiration. 'For we walk by faith, not by sight', or 'appearance'.[4]

In his day Martin Luther asserted concerning the doctrine of sinners' justification before God by faith in Jesus Christ, that it is the article of the Christian faith by which the Church

[1] Eph. ii. 4–6 [2] Zc. vi. 12, 13
[3] See Rom. vi. 8–13; Eph. iv. 20–24; Col. ii. 20–iii. 11
[4] 2 Cor. v. 7, and RV mg.

stands or falls. For the Church as one body, like every individual sinner who by grace finds his place within it, can stand accepted in God's sight only by faith in Christ alone. And if the Church cannot stand there, it is fallen indeed, no matter how the visible earthly Church may stand either in men's eyes or in its own.

The sinner who is justified by faith in Christ enjoys three complementary benefits. First, he gains immediate and permanent acceptance in God's sight as righteous. Second, he gains freedom of access to God's presence in the liberty of the God-given Spirit who enables him, without fear, to call God 'Father'. Third, he gains the thrilling prospect of an ultimate share in the glory of full redemption and perfected holiness.[1]

The same three benefits are similarly granted corporately to the community of the justified. First, the Church, all who belong to it, are together presented 'holy and unblameable and unreproveable in his sight'.[2] For the true Church, in spite of all the conscious sinfulness of its members at present on earth, stands before God in Christ justified. Second, the Church, particularly its members at present on earth, is called to realize the benefit of its standing in grace and of its indwelling by the Spirit, in freely drawing near to God in worship and prayer. Christians enter fully into the present privileges of their Church membership only when they thus come to the throne of grace—to mount Zion, to the heavenly Jerusalem, to their high priest upon the throne—in order to join in the communion of the saints in worship, and to obtain grace for immediate earthly needs.[3] Third, the Church is destined to share corporately, as the bride of Christ, in the coming crowning day of glory, when the manifested Lord will own the Church as His, and 'present it to himself a glorious church, not having spot, or wrinkle, or any such thing'.[4] Christians should be inspired to endure present suffering for Christ's sake, by reckoning that 'the sufferings of this present time are not worthy to be compared with the glory which shall be revealed in us'.[5]

[1] See Rom. v. 1, 2, 5, viii. 15
[2] Col. i. 22
[3] See Heb. iv. 16, viii. 1, xii. 22–24
[4] See Eph. v. 25–27
[5] Rom. viii. 18

These truths about the Church are wholly unseen and partly future. They are not discernible by the natural senses. They are the very kind of values with which faith deals, for 'faith is the substance of things hoped for, the evidence of things not seen'.[1] Such truths, therefore, are rightly confessed by faith, as they are, for instance, in the historic creeds. For the one holy Church, the *una sancta ecclesia*, is not an object of sight. But to Christian believers it is an object of faith. For we believe that this is how the Church is reckoned now in God's sight; it is presented 'faultless'. And we believe that this is what it will actually and inherently be made in outworked perfection in the coming crowning day of final glorification, 'not having spot, or wrinkle, or any such thing'.[2]

This awareness of faith concerning the one holy Church of God, in whose present acceptance with God, and in whose final perfection in God, we thus believe, must also influence our attitude both to the visible Church militant here on earth, and to the local congregations to which we individually belong. For, at its largest, in any one generation the Church militant here on earth is only a minority of the one saved community. The one true Church includes the vast number of departed saints. It also includes in God's mind those who are yet to be added to complete the number of God's elect. And of those who belong to the visible Church on earth it includes only the 'faithful in Christ Jesus'[3] (i.e., the true believers), and not all the professing members. So, in distinction from the visible Church or churches, the one true Church, known fully only to God and discernible by us only by faith, may rightly be called 'invisible', just as God Himself is called invisible[4] although His presence and activity and our living relation to Him may be life's biggest realities.

When Martin Luther looked at himself and at the life he lived before the eyes of men, he was compelled to qualify his awareness of being justified in God's sight. He described himself as *simul iustus et peccator*, that is, 'at one and the same time

[1] Heb. xi. 1 [2] Eph. v. 27 [3] Eph. i. 1
[4] See Heb. xi. 27; cf. 1 Pet. i. 8

justified and a sinner'. The same qualification has to be added in description of the Church militant here on earth. It is reckoned as perfect in Christ before God. It has to be recognized as very imperfect on earth before men. Indeed, because only a minority of the members of the one true Church is on earth at any one time, and because they are still in a sinful environment, and themselves frequently guilty of sinning, the full perfection of the Church of God is unrealizable here. The mature manhood of the Church, 'the measure of the stature of the fulness of Christ'[1] is a goal finally to be realized only in the consummation of the life beyond, after the resurrection of the body, with the number of the elect complete, and with the faithful no longer mixed with the unbelieving. We ought not, therefore, to hope and work for an achievement in this world which, according to the purposes and providence of God, can be realized only in the life beyond.

Yet in spite of all the limitations and qualifications necessarily besetting any visible, earthly manifestation of the Church, it is most significant that to describe one local congregation of professed believers in Christ, both our Lord and the writers of the New Testament used the unqualified name 'the church';[2] and sometimes St. Paul uses the explicitly theological description 'the church of God',[3] or ' the church of the Thessalonians in God our Father and the Lord Jesus Christ'.[4] Such a description indicates that what is thus locally constituted, and made visible and functioning, is genuine 'church'. One may find a suggestive illustration in our common method of reference to the moon. When one sees a thin crescent only in the sky, one says, not 'There is a part of the moon', but 'There is the moon'. For the small part that is visible is genuine moon; and, what is more, it is actually, though to us invisibly, united with all the rest of the moon.

Similarly, a local Christian congregation—indeed, as our Lord went on to indicate, even two or three gathered together in His name with Christ Himself in the midst of them[5]—is

[1] Eph. iv. 13
[2] Mt. xviii. 17; 1 Cor. xiv. 19, 23
[3] 1 Cor. i. 2; 2 Cor. i. 1
[4] 2 Thes. i. 1; cf. 1 Thes. i. 1
[5] See Mt. xviii. 20

genuine 'church' become visible. It is, as St. Paul says of the local group of Christians at Corinth, essentially 'body of Christ',[1] and invisibly one in Him with the whole of His body, the Church. It is this awareness of belonging to the one invisible Church that gives participation in its local visible manifestation its full significance. If, therefore, in our realization of Church unity and Christian fellowship, we are to be not only truly catholic and ecumenical, but also properly spiritual and Christian, we need first of all an awareness by faith of the unseen reality of the communion of the saints.

Next we must notice the significant fact that, when local congregations of Christians are referred to in the New Testament, they are not collectively called 'the Church'; that is, they are not thought of as constituent parts of one organized earthly institution. Rather, they are explicitly and surprisingly called, in the plural, 'the churches', and even 'the churches of God'. For example, in the Revelation John does not write, 'He who has an ear, let him hear what the Spirit says to the Church', but '. . . what the Spirit saith unto the churches'.[2] Similarly St. Paul, when giving guidance about the veiling of women in the congregation, does not say dogmatically (as some today would like to talk), 'The Church has no such practice', but 'If any one is disposed to be contentious, we recognize no other practice, nor do the churches of God'.[3]

Nor in the New Testament writings is any earthly centre regarded as the official headquarters or metropolis of the Church on earth. The only city which could possibly make such a claim in apostolic times was Jerusalem. Yet the evidence reveals that the wider missionary movement in the Roman world outside Palestine, with all its far-reaching consequences for the spread of the gospel and the growth of the Church, was promoted by the Spirit through the local and very independent church at Antioch,[4] not through the church of

[1] 1 Cor. xii. 27. The Greek nouns have no articles. The one congregation is not 'the body of Christ'; but it is generically 'body of Christ'.

[2] Rev. ii. 7 [3] 1 Cor. xi. 16, RSV [4] See Acts xiii. 1–3, xiv. 26, 27

Jerusalem. Indeed, influences from Jerusalem tended rather deliberately to oppose and radically to corrupt the obvious work of the Spirit of God. In consequence, St. Paul, stirred to write to his converts in Galatia to denounce these influences, goes into detailed personal testimony concerning his conversion to Christ, his apostleship, and the gospel which he preached, in order to demonstrate his complete independence of Jerusalem, and, indeed, the need on occasion to withstand pressure from those in Jerusalem in the interests of nothing less than the truth of the gospel itself.[1] In addition, the Church council held at Jerusalem to consider such matters decided, under the guidance of the Spirit, to disown the requirements for membership in the saved community which some from Judaea and Jerusalem were trying to impose on the Church.[2] And in his letter to the Galatian Christians the apostle Paul explicitly disowns the earthly Jerusalem as a place of bondage.[3] Christians, particularly Hebrew Christians, are told plainly 'We have not here an abiding city, but we seek after the city which is to come'.[4] Christians ought, therefore, to find the proper focus for their love and loyalty in 'the Jerusalem which is above'. For she is, as St. Paul declares, the one *free* city, and our only true metropolis, 'the mother of us all'.[5]

The Jews, of course, regarded Jerusalem on earth as their holy city. The scattered groups of Jews, meeting locally in synagogues in many places of the known world, regarded themselves as Jews of the Dispersion,[6] whose true mother-city was Jerusalem. Similarly, in the political world of the Roman Empire, the mother-city was Rome, and the great and coveted privilege in society was to be a Roman citizen.[7] Many places scattered throughout the Roman world, Philippi for example, were (or more strictly had sojourning in them) Roman colonies, whose members were citizens of Rome.[8] Such citizens looked to Rome as their great metropolis; they could, as Paul did, appeal direct to Caesar.[9]

[1] See Gal. i. 1–ii. 10
[2] See Acts xv. 1, 24
[3] Gal. iv. 25, 30
[4] Heb. xiii. 14, RV
[5] Gal. iv. 26
[6] See Jn. vii. 35
[7] See Acts xxii. 25–28
[8] See Acts xvi. 21
[9] See Acts xxv. 8–12

In the affairs of the Christian churches there was a similarity with a significant difference. The local churches were, like synagogues of the Dispersion, scattered away from their holy city in a foreign land.[1] They were like colonies overseas whose members were citizens of the imperial city. But, for them, no earthly city like Jerusalem, or no local church like the church in Rome, could claim the high privilege of being the Christians' metropolis. For their commonwealth or citizenship was in heaven;[2] their mother-city was the heavenly Jerusalem. The Head, the High-priest, the King to whom they looked, or could appeal, was no earthly prelate or emperor, but the exalted Lord enthroned at God's right hand.

These truths still have their pertinent and practical application to our own earthly sojourn and pilgrimage as Christian believers. Here we have no continuing city, no visible human head. We are called to go forth unto Jesus as our one rallying-centre, as our only sovereign Lord, the one true 'Shepherd and Bishop'[3] of our souls, the only proper 'chief Shepherd',[4] or archbishop, of the local pastors and elders. Each local congregation, indeed each individual believer, must maintain direct vital communion with the Head, and come continually in the Spirit to the heavenly mount Zion.[5]

Christian unity is thus meant to be realized and expressed before men, not as the creation of human organization, but as the proper function and fulfilment of a spiritual organism divinely directed by its single Head. Nor can true Christian fellowship be established and extended more widely by bureaucratic centralization and efficiency, but only by believers actually meeting together. This they can do invisibly in the Spirit at the throne of grace, as they come to the heavenly mount Zion. This they can do visibly in the flesh by coming together in actual localized meetings, whether it be in a regular gathering or congregation of local residents in any particular neighbourhood, or in a special gathering or conference of Christians assembled from far and near.

[1] See 1 Pet. i. 1
[2] See Phil. iii. 20, RV and mg.
[3] 1 Pet. ii. 25
[4] 1 Pet. v. 4
[5] See Col. ii. 16–19; Heb. xii. 22–29

A danger of our day seems to be lest Christians become wrongly persuaded that more effective world-wide co-operation of scattered congregations can be achieved from some earthly centre, and through some extraordinary human leadership. The truth is that the Christian secret of true unity is unique, and holds promise of supernatural success just because it is unlike all such human organization. Indeed, it is wrong for Christians to think they need a human president or king, like earthly states and empires, when Christ Himself is our King. In addition, we can enter fully into the realized and manifested unity of the Spirit, as distinct from organizational integration, only as each believer or each local congregation is directed by the one Lord and not by some earthly General Headquarters or Commander-in-chief. Our need is not to heed what the great world Church says to her members, but rather for every individual believer in his own local congregation to hear direct what the Spirit says to the churches.

There is, therefore, no scriptural ground for looking for the emergence of one ecumenical or world-wide Church as a visible earthly organization, having, like an earthly empire, a geographical centre and a human head. The great invisible Church's one mother-city is the heavenly Zion, not Rome, nor Canterbury, nor Geneva. The great invisible Church's one Head is Christ Himself, not some human pope, nor primate, nor moderator. True Christian loyalists, or as we may call them, proper biblical churchmen, believe in, and not a few have been prepared to die for, the Crown Rights of the Redeemer.

III. PRESENT OUTWORKING

CHAPTER EIGHT

EVANGELISM AND WORLD-WIDE EXPANSION

THE primary task given to the company of His followers by the risen Lord, before His ascension into heaven, was the task of making the gospel known to the ends of the earth. World-wide evangelism, therefore, was from the first, and still is, the chief task of the Church militant here on earth, in order that the elect community, which Christ died to redeem, may continually be added to, and ultimately made complete.

Jesus explicitly taught that the purpose of His death and resurrection as God's Christ was to make it possible for an opportunity of repentance, and the benefit of remission of sins, to be offered to, and embraced by, men of all nations. He also indicated that He expected His followers to become the world-wide propagators of this gospel. So, for instance, we read:

> Then opened he their understanding, that they might understand the scriptures, and said unto them, Thus it is written, and thus it behoved Christ to suffer, and to rise from the dead the third day: and that repentance and remission of sins should be preached in his name among all nations, beginning at Jerusalem.[1]
> And he said unto them, Go ye into all the world, and preach the gospel to every creature.[2]

Examination will show that every one of the four Gospel records ends, and that the Acts of the Apostles begins, with direct mention of this expectation of our Lord. Since such repetition itself suggests importance, let us quote again:

> And he said unto them, . . . But ye shall receive power, after that the Holy Ghost is come upon you: and ye shall be witnesses unto me both in Jerusalem, and in all Judaea, and in Samaria, and unto the uttermost part of the earth.[3]

[1] Lk. xxiv. 45–47 [2] Mk. xvi. 15 [3] Acts i. 7, 8

The evidence compels us to recognize that Jesus Himself gave to His followers an authoritative commission to discharge this task of evangelism, and that He promised always His own enabling presence as the all-powerful Lord to sustain them in the doing of it.[1]

This commission was given, in the first place, to the eleven apostles. They had enjoyed unique privileges. They had companied with Jesus throughout His ministry. They had seen Him after His resurrection from the dead. They were, in consequence, made responsible to bear witness to these things. The faith of the whole Church is built upon, and governed by, their testimony and teaching. Only by the maintenance of steadfast loyalty to the apostles' doctrine[2] can the Church be truly 'apostolic'.

On the other hand, the records of St. Luke and of St. John suggest, when carefully examined and compared, that this commission to preach the gospel was undoubtedly given by our Lord to the larger company of His disciples and not to the eleven alone. Had He not, during His ministry, in anticipation of this, sent out seventy to preach[3] as well as the twelve? In the historic creeds we rightly confess that the whole Church is 'apostolic'; and this description can be understood partly in this sense, that the whole Church shares in the God-given task and responsibility of being 'sent' to preach the gospel.

This wider application of our Lord's words particularly applies to the relevant passage in the Fourth Gospel. There we read:

> The same day at evening, being the first day of the week, when the doors were shut where the disciples were assembled for fear of the Jews, came Jesus and stood in the midst, and saith unto them . . . Peace be unto you: as my Father hath sent me, even so send I you. And when he had said this, he breathed on them, and saith unto them, Receive ye the Holy Ghost: whose soever sins ye remit, they are remitted unto them; and whose soever sins ye retain, they are retained.[4]

Comparison of this passage with those at the end of the other

[1] See Mt. xxviii. 18–20
[2] See Acts ii. 42
[3] See Lk. x. 1ff.
[4] Jn. xx. 19–23

three Gospel records compels the recognition that the words about the remission or retention of sins refer to the preaching of the gospel and its far-reaching consequences. By such words our Lord indicated that the faithful preacher shares in a ministry by which men's eternal destiny is settled. Those hearers who, through such preaching, believe in the Person and work of Christ find eternal forgiveness. Those hearers who reject this offer involve themselves in a guilt and a condemnation from which there is no other way of salvation. In so far, therefore, as these words of our Lord suggest the conveyance of a power to give to the responsive hearer priestly absolution, this power is to be recognized as being employed, not by a select class of 'priests' only, but by any Christian who, in the exercise of the priesthood which belongs to all the redeemed people of God, assures repentant sinners, who trust in Christ and His saving work, of the absolution of the gospel. They are forgiven.

If we now turn our attention to the Acts of the Apostles, we find that the dominant interest of this single New Testament record of the history of the early Church is an interest in evangelism and in world-wide expansion. The record also makes repeatedly and unmistakably clear that in all this activity and development the decisive initiative lies, not with the twelve apostles, nor with the mother church at Jerusalem, but with the Holy Ghost, and with the different human agents whom the Spirit is pleased to use.

In the record itself the twelve apostles and the Jerusalem church soon cease to be prominent. Developments occurred which the twelve apostles were slow to appreciate and to accept as of God, let alone to promote of their own accord. Stephen, and those who through his preaching were led to share his insight, were clearly ahead of the apostles in discerning that the new gospel of Christ meant that the old order of the ceremonial law and of the local temple in Jerusalem had had its day.[1] When Stephen paid for the expression of

[1] See Acts vi. 9–14

such convictions with his blood, and Christians who shared such convictions were persecuted and had to flee from Jerusalem, Luke records:

> And at that time there was a great persecution against the church which was at Jerusalem; and they were all scattered abroad throughout the regions of Judaea and Samaria, except the apostles.[1]

Why 'except the apostles'? Is this a hint that the apostles, far from being the first, were the last to become propagators of these evangelical truths?

Luke then records extension to Samaria, and the conversion to faith in Christ of an Ethiopian eunuch, not through the apostles, but through Philip, a man led of the Spirit. The apostles, still 'at Jerusalem'[2] and not out doing wider preaching, sent Peter and John to investigate these new developments in Samaria. Manifest signs among the new converts of the presence of the Holy Spirit persuaded them that this new extension was of God. So on their return journey they, too, 'preached the gospel in many villages of the Samaritans'.[3] Nevertheless they 'returned to Jerusalem', instead of going further afield. So Luke next records[4] how the risen Lord Himself, by a unique personal appearance from the glory of the heavens, and wholly independently of any action of the twelve apostles and the Jerusalem church, brings Saul the persecutor to acknowledge Him as Lord, and constitutes him a new additional apostle who, by the risen Lord's direct personal call and commission, is to do the work the twelve seem to have been slow to do, and to be the great pioneer of wider Gentile evangelism. Again, the apostles and other members of the Jerusalem church are shown to be hesitant. Luke records:

> And when Saul was come to Jerusalem, he assayed to join himself to the disciples: but they were all afraid of him, and believed not that he was a disciple.[5]

The man who saw a work of God's Spirit in Saul, and per-

[1] Acts viii. 1
[2] Acts viii. 14
[3] See Acts viii. 14–25
[4] Acts ix. 1ff.
[5] Acts ix. 26

suaded the apostles to accept him as a true convert, was not one of the twelve, but Barnabas.[1]

Peter is next shown to be on the move, and active in the power of God among the saints and disciples in places other than Jerusalem;[2] but, against his inherited Jewish preferences, supported, as they were, by strong religious sanctions of the old order, he has to be literally compelled by the Spirit to go to the Gentile household of Cornelius and there preach the gospel of Christ. It was the Spirit, given direct to his believing hearers by the exalted Lord, independently of any action or acceptance of them on his part, that persuaded Peter that God had added them to the saved community, and that he must openly confirm their admission to membership in the Church by administering Christian baptism.[3]

Developments also took place at Antioch in Syria, which were wholly independent of the twelve apostles and the Jerusalem church. The gospel was preached freely to Greeks,[4] that is, to Gentiles who had no previous connection at all with Judaism and its ceremonialism. This preaching was blessed of God. 'And the hand of the Lord was with them', we read: 'and a great number believed, and turned unto the Lord.'[5] The church in Jerusalem had misgivings about all this; at least they felt its character must be investigated. The man they trusted, as quick to discern the new and unexpected in the ways of the risen Lord and the quickening Spirit, was Barnabas, not one of the twelve. He at once recognized the grace of God in what was happening; 'and much people was added unto the Lord'.[6]

It was this independent congregation at Antioch, the independent convert and 'irregular' apostle Saul, and the spiritually sensitive Barnabas, who, under the providence of God, were now brought together, and used by the Spirit to promote much larger expansion to the wider Gentile world.[7] In this connection St. Paul confesses in his letter to the Galatians how he felt the need to reassure himself that what he was

[1] See Acts ix. 27 [2] Acts ix. 32–43 [3] Acts x
[4] Acts xi. 19, 20, RV [5] Acts xi. 21 [6] See Acts xi. 22–24
[7] See Acts xi. 25, 26, xiii. 1–4, xiv. 26–28

preaching to the Gentiles, the gospel of salvation by grace, through faith in Christ alone, without any necessary ceremonies, was acknowledged by the so-called 'pillars' of the church in Jerusalem as complete, and not fatally deficient.[1] Not that Paul himself had any doubts. It was to him nothing less than 'the truth of the gospel' that was at stake. He would not yield to pressure to accept ritual ceremonies and legal observances as necessary to salvation, 'no, not for an hour'. But he was painfully aware that wrong influences from Jerusalem could easily and grievously interfere with the success of his work of Gentile evangelism.[2] The Church leaders, whom he saw in Jerusalem, James, Cephas and John, fully acknowledged, he says, his God-given apostleship. They did not regard his gospel as incomplete in any essential. 'They added nothing to me', says Paul; in terms, that is, either of ordination or orthodoxy.[3]

The twentieth-century Church has still much to learn from these New Testament records. What should be decisive in the counsels and activities of the Church is the initiative of the Spirit, and the perception of the grace of God given unto men, particularly to those who exercise any kind of ministry. For there is real danger still lest long-established mother-churches, in countries from which the gospel has been carried to other lands, should through their leaders exert an improper prestige influence or, by their excessive and limited devotion to certain forms of worship and of church order, prove unwilling to recognize that the one Spirit of God may do His work of baptizing outsiders into Christ, and of building them up in His body, without the necessary use of any of these forms. On this issue, let us notice, the apostle Paul was very pointedly outspoken. He withstood Peter to the face, because he 'walked not uprightly according to the truth of the gospel'.[4] He says of those 'who were reputed to be pillars', and whose persons and position consequently tended to carry weight in

[1] See Gal. ii. 1–10 [2] See Gal. ii. 3–5 [3] Gal. ii. 6–10
[4] See Gal. ii. 11–14

conference: 'whatsoever they were, it maketh no matter to me: God accepteth no man's person'.[1]

When dissension was caused among the churches of Gentile converts to Christ, particularly at Antioch by certain men from Judaea, who taught that circumcision was necessary to salvation, a deputation went to Jerusalem to the apostles and elders there, to seek to settle the question.[2] The council which consequently assembled was persuaded of the truth of God in the matter, not by the leadership of men, but by the undeniable initiative of the Spirit of God. Having heard Peter's testimony about his experience in the house of Cornelius, James rightly deduced that the first and decisive action in this matter was taken by God, not by Peter or any other man.[3] It was, therefore, of their wisdom as a council to follow the divine leading. So they significantly wrote, 'it seemed good to the Holy Ghost, and to us'.[4]

It is high time that in some quarters today there was a fresh willingness to acknowledge that, if it has seemed good to the Spirit of God to work in saving and sanctifying power in congregations and through ministries different in their ways and character from our own, it ought also to seem good unto us not to trouble our fellow-Christians with doctrines and demands, whose acceptance is clearly not essential to salvation in Christ, and to living communion with Him.

In order to further such evangelism and world-wide expansion of the Church as we are here considering, the primary ministry is obviously preaching. When our Lord chose twelve that they might be with Him as disciples, to learn of Him, His ultimate intention was to send them forth to preach.[5] This is how they became 'apostles', by being sent forth.[6] The great concern of their apostleship was 'to preach the gospel'.[7]

When St. Paul mentions the special ministers given by the ascended Lord 'for the perfecting of the saints', and 'for the edifying of the body of Christ', he says that first 'he gave some,

[1] Gal. ii. 6–9 [2] Acts xv. 1, 2ff.
[3] Cf. Acts xv. 14, 'how first God' (RV) [4] Acts xv. 28
[5] Mk. iii. 14 [6] See Mk. vi. 7, 30 [7] See 1 Cor. i. 17

apostles; and some, prophets; and some, evangelists'.[1] These three types are all directly concerned with the ministry of the word. Apostles and prophets were special gifts to the primitive Church. They are spoken of as the Church's 'foundation'.[2] They were the men to whom, by the Spirit, revelation was given of the full content and meaning of what St. Paul describes as

> the mystery of Christ, which in other ages was not made known unto the sons of men, as it is now revealed unto his holy apostles and prophets by the Spirit.[3]

Such special ministries, essential at the beginning, have not been perpetuated in the Church. But the way in which Paul places 'evangelists' immediately after them and before 'pastors and teachers' indicates how, in a more permanent way throughout subsequent Church history, the preaching of the gospel is fundamental to the very continuance of the Church, and to the continual adding to it, by the Lord, of those who are being saved.

St. Paul's exhortation later to Timothy to 'do the work of an evangelist'[4] indicates in its context how important it is that anyone who is largely occupied with the pastoral care of the churches should still regard evangelism as an essential part of full ministry. For only if nominal members—particularly second and third generation Christians—are brought to living faith in Christ through active evangelistic preaching within the congregation will vital Church membership be properly sustained. And to reach those completely outside the Church who are without any knowledge of God in Christ the great need is certainly for evangelists—men who will preach Christ and the gospel, whether to the crowd or to the individual.[5] For, as St. Paul indicates, it is the word of faith preached which brings God in Christ so near to men that all that men have to do to obtain salvation is to believe in the heart, and to confess with the mouth, that Jesus is their living and exalted Lord—able to save all who call upon Him.[6]

[1] Eph. iv. 11, 12 [2] Eph. ii. 20 [3] Eph. iii. 3–5
[4] 2 Tim. iv. 5 [5] See Acts viii. 5, 35 [6] See Rom. x. 6–13

But such decisive response to Christ and the gospel will not be made unless preachers are sent to enable men to hear and to believe. So St. Paul continues:

> How then shall they call on him in whom they have not believed? and how shall they believe in him of whom they have not heard? and how shall they hear without a preacher? And how shall they preach, except they be sent?[1]

In the Greek the word 'sent' is here literally 'apostolized', or made 'apostles' or 'missionaries'. This is how Barnabas and Saul went to Cyprus and South Galatia from the church in Antioch, 'being sent forth by the Holy Ghost'.[2] It is such preachers of the gospel who constitute the primary apostolic ministry, and the indispensable apostolic succession in the life and witness of the Church of God. Without them the gospel would never be carried to the ends of the earth. Theirs is the work which is peculiarly beautiful or virtuous in God's sight.

> As it is written, How beautiful are the feet of them that preach the gospel of peace, and bring glad tidings of good things![3]

It is time that this was recognized worthily in the churches. For there is a widespread tendency to regard 'pastors and teachers' in the local churches, particularly if they are called 'bishops' or 'presbyters', as having a status as ministers in the Church of God superior to that of evangelists and missionaries, particularly any who may have had no similar church 'ordination'. This is not, as we see it, a proper New Testament standard of reckoning.

There is, therefore, fundamental scriptural justification for believing and confessing that the one true Church of God is called to be both apostolic and catholic, sharing, that is, in a missionary commission whose discharge will make its membership embrace men and women from all races and ages of the world. This goal of God's purpose for His people, this calling of the saved community in Christ, will be entered into and worked out by us, in our day and generation, only if we are in vision and in venture truly missionary-hearted and ecumenical in our evangelistic zeal.

[1] Rom. x. 14, 15 [2] Acts xiii. 4 [3] Rom. x. 15

At this point I feel constrained to add that I thank God for the many Christian groups active today, particularly among students and young people, whose dominant interests are evangelism at home and the reaching of the unevangelized with the gospel in all parts of the world. If it has seemed good to the Spirit of God to raise them up, and so markedly to use their witness, ought it not to seem good to us to acknowledge them as of God? Even if, understandably, they seem to some to be born out of due time, or to function in an improper way, ought they not to be recognized as gifts of the ascended Lord to His Church, to do the work which the established churches and their leaders have been slow to face, particularly because of the latter's excessive readiness to treat nominal and baptized church members as if they were all genuine Christians, born of God's Spirit? But of this more in our next chapter.

CHAPTER NINE

CHURCH MEMBERSHIP

ALL who are familiar with both Bible and Church history must acknowledge that there is, and long has been, in the world a visible community or distinguishable company of people, known in Old Testament times as Israel, and known since the days of our Lord as the Church. Just as circumcision and participation in the passover were special outward signs of membership in the one, so Christian baptism and participation in the Lord's supper are special outward signs of membership in the other. When any number of these members meet together as a congregation to engage in distinctive religious activity, it has been, and still is, an important feature of their practice to profess in various ways that the Lord is their God and that they are His people.

It is, however, equally plain from the evidence both of Scripture and of experience that this professing community or Church of God, whether it be thought of universally as all Israel, or the Church militant here on earth, or whether it be thought of locally as assembled in a single congregation, is unquestionably a mixed community. While all are nominal members, not all are genuine sharers in the truths to which their distinct existence bears witness. While all are visible participants in acts of worship and fellowship, not all are in true, living communion with God in Christ. It is this necessary distinction and its far-reaching implications that we now intend to consider.

Let us notice first, from the teaching of our Lord and of the New Testament, three ways in which the visible community tends to be mixed and not wholly pure in its membership. The first cause of such mixture is the very character of the invitation of the gospel of saving grace. By it, all who are willing to respond are invited to come, and are promised full personal participation in God-given benefits simply by coming, by believing and receiving. Jesus Himself indicated explicitly, particularly in some of His parables, that this kind of method and appeal was bound to procure a 'mixed bag'. For instance, He said:

> The kingdom of heaven is like unto a net, that was cast into the sea, and gathered of every kind: which, when it was full, they drew to shore, and sat down, and gathered the good into vessels, but cast the bad away. So shall it be at the end of the world: the angels shall come forth, and sever the wicked from among the just.[1]

Or again, in the parable of the wedding feast prepared by a king for his son, when those first bidden to come refused to do so, the king said to his servants:

> Go ye therefore into the highways, and as many as ye shall find, bid to the marriage. So those servants went out into the highways, and gathered together all as many as they found, both bad and good: and the wedding was furnished with guests.[2]

We may at once appreciate here, in direct relation to the invitation of Christ in the gospel, how individuals may come, not only with varying degrees of understanding, but also with very varied motives. In the case of some it may really be for selfish and material ends and not in order to find peace with God or to embrace spiritual aid with the aim of growing in personal holiness. This truth needs to be remembered not least by those active in evangelism, some of whom are much too prone to count, at once, as genuine converts to Christ all who openly respond.

When our Lord Himself gathered around Him a company of personal adherents or disciples, He did not at once treat them all as being genuine and whole-hearted in their response. He pointedly and pertinently stressed, with vivid, dramatic illustration, the fundamental difference among professed disciples between what He called the wise and the foolish. He indicated first their similarity, a similarity which united them.

[1] Mt. xiii. 47–49 [2] Mt. xxii. 9, 10

All alike were hearers of His teaching, all were professed disciples, all were members of a single distinguishable company. He then indicated their significant difference, a difference which ultimately must decisively divide them. For, in the day of testing and of judgment, the one kind would stand, and the other kind would fall.[1]

Jesus also plainly taught that professed adherence to Himself and actual, sustained participation in some of the distinctive activities of His followers were no necessary guarantee of genuineness and of final acceptance in God's sight. To some who will say, 'We have eaten and drunk in thy presence, and thou hast taught in our streets', the master of the house, who has shut the door, and left them outside, will answer, 'I tell you, I know you not whence ye are; depart from me, all ye workers of iniquity'.[2]

From our Lord's own teaching we thus learn that what matters is not merely acknowledgement of Jesus as Lord, and participation in work publicly done in His name. Accompanying this there must also be the practice of obedience to God's will, and the experience of knowing personally, and being known by, the Lord Himself. These are His words:

> Not every one that saith unto me, Lord, Lord, shall enter into the kingdom of heaven; but he that doeth the will of my Father which is in heaven. Many will say to me in that day, Lord, Lord, have we not prophesied in thy name? and in thy name have cast out devils? and in thy name done many wonderful works? And then will I profess unto them, I never knew you: depart from me, ye that work iniquity.[3]

The same two decisive criteria by which the true Church, which the Lord has founded and is building, is to be distinguished from nominal members of the visible community (and particularly, as both contexts indicate, from false prophets) are reiterated in reverse order by St. Paul, when he wrote:

> Nevertheless the foundation of God standeth sure, having this seal, The Lord knoweth them that are his. And, Let every one that nameth the name of Christ depart from iniquity.[4]

[1] See Mt. vii. 24–27 [2] See Lk. xiii. 23–30 [3] Mt. vii. 21–23
[4] 2 Tim. ii. 19

The second cause of the radical mixture in character of the membership of the visible earthly community is the activity of the great enemy of God, the devil himself. Our Lord, after depicting Himself in a parable (according to His own interpretation) as sowing in the field of the world the good seed of 'the children of the kingdom', also spoke of His enemy, the devil, who sowed, among the wheat, tares, that is, 'children of the wicked one'.[1] This illustration also suggests that the tares would grow so close alongside the wheat, and, particularly in their early stages, would be so similar in appearance and profession, that it would be impossible even for true servants of our Lord successfully to root them out. If they tried to do so, the danger would be that they would root out the wheat with them. The necessary separation, Jesus taught, would in due time be done at His command, not now but later, and by angels not men.

In this parable, at a time in His ministry when our Lord seems to have been facing, and revealing, the somewhat unexpected ways in which He knew His work in the world was to find fulfilment, He thus plainly warns His followers that admixture of this wholly evil kind will inevitably appear in the very midst of the visible community. The 'children of the wicked one', as He called them, are clearly individuals whose hearts are not right with God, men wholly given up to wrong interests and ambitions.

The greatest and most sobering illustration of this very truth is to be found in the presence of Judas Iscariot among our Lord's twelve disciples. Because of it Jesus said, 'Have not I chosen you twelve, and one of you is a devil?'[2] This man, far from being a 'son of the kingdom', is classified as 'the son of perdition'.[3] In the outworking of his personal relation to Jesus he is seen to be not one whom the Spirit could use to confess Christ, but one into whom the devil could, and did, enter to cause him to betray Christ.[4]

In His teaching our Lord also revealed some aspects of the devil's strategy in this connection. The unclean spirit may

[1] See Mt. xiii. 24–30, 36–43 [2] Jn. vi. 70 [3] Jn. xvii. 12
[4] See Jn. xiii. 2, 27

temporarily go out of a man without renouncing ownership. This permits reformation, but not regeneration. The individual concerned may temporarily join in, and outwardly conform to, some standard Christian activity, so that he professes and appears to be one of Christ's followers. But all is done without any true personal renunciation of evil or any liberating and regenerating experience of the lordship of Christ. The result is that a day comes when the evil spirit says:

> I will return into my house from whence I came out; and when he is come, he findeth it empty, swept, and garnished. Then goeth he, and taketh with himself seven other spirits more wicked than himself, and they enter in and dwell there: and the last state of that man is worse than the first.[1]

Nor will a generation come in the history of the Church militant here on earth when it can expect to be completely free from such grievous mixture. Jesus Himself said that the wheat and the tares are thus to be allowed to grow together until the harvest, until the Son of man uses His angels to separate them at the end of present world history.[2]

The third cause of the mixture in the membership of the present visible community is the presence in it of nominal 'sons of the kingdom', whose ultimate destiny will be to be 'cast out', as not genuine heirs of the promised inheritance.[3] In our Lord's day there were Jews, particularly zealous religious Jews like the Pharisees, whose boast was that they were sons of Abraham. They thought that they already belonged to the kingdom of God by birth, by special personal heritage and privilege, and by participation in decisive distinguishing ordinances, like circumcision. They denied that they were bondslaves needing to be freed.[4] Therefore they had no readiness of spirit to repent and believe the gospel; they had no self-humiliation as sinners before God. In consequence Jesus plainly warned them that the publicans and the harlots, and Gentiles from distant lands, would go into the kingdom of

[1] Mt. xii. 43–45
[2] See Mt. xiii. 24–30, 36–43
[3] See Mt. viii. 12; Gal. iv. 30
[4] See Jn. viii. 33

God before them, and that they themselves would be cast out.[1]

Later, in the Epistles, we find that St. Paul referred in the same way to the Judaizers, who troubled his Gentile converts. He said that they were 'born after the flesh',[2] and that they were in the bondage of legalism and ceremonialism. They were not 'born after the Spirit', and set free in Christ. Yet they claimed to belong to the Church. Indeed, they not only expected to exercise outwardly the privileges of membership; they also claimed by their very ceremonialism to set the pattern of full and proper membership. But the apostle says emphatically that they are to be distinguished from the true seed of Abraham, and that, as the written word witnesses, their ultimate destiny is to be cast out. 'Nevertheless', he writes, 'what saith the scripture? Cast out the bondwoman and her son: for the son of the bondwoman shall not be heir with the son of the freewoman.'[3]

It is important that we should not be unwilling to recognize the same kind of mixture in the visible Church of our day. This particularly applies in a land where the profession of Christianity is a long-established heritage, and where it is easy to assume that one belongs 'according to the flesh', just by natural birth and upbringing, and by participation in Church ordinances.[4] Many are prone to feel that all is well because they can say: we have the Church as our mother. She gave us the baptism by which we became Christians. And (so some can add) we ourselves are active church members and regular communicants. So, nominally, without question they are 'sons of the kingdom'; and this is how they are (and to some extent must be) commonly treated and addressed. Yet without repentance, without true faith in Christ and His saving work, and without new birth of the Spirit, they must eventually be cast out—by the Lord, not by men. This is the teaching of our Lord and of the New Testament.

Over against this assertion it is claimed by some that in those New Testament Epistles which are addressed to local churches,

[1] See Mt. xxi. 28–32, viii. 11, 12 [2] See Gal. iv. 29 [3] Gal. iv. 30
[4] See Phil. iii. 3–9

the writers regard all the members as genuine Christians, and make no such radical distinction between the nominal and the genuine. There is a measure of truth in this claim. Men who make a profession of being Christians, and who have a properly ordered, formal claim to having been admitted to the Church (for example, by baptism), must all in certain ways be treated as being in fact what they are in name. This applies the more to this matter of Church membership because our Lord's teaching explicitly forbids us to try to divide those who make the same profession of faith, on the grounds that we think some are genuine and others are not. For no man has the ability infallibly to distinguish good from bad in this way.

It is by the presence or absence in men's lives of the fruit of true Christian good works that more objective ground is provided for making possible distinction between the genuine and the merely nominal Christians. But such distinction cannot be made by a writer or preacher addressing a local church as a whole. He must address them in the light of what they all profess to be. Also, the significant positive truth about the professing visible Church, mixed as it is in character, is that it is the sphere within which God is pleased specially to work, and the sphere within which genuine members of Christ are normally to be found. It is to them that language such as that of some New Testament Epistles fully applies.

To use the Old Testament language in illustration, as the New Testament writers sometimes do, we may say that, while 'they are not all Israel, which are of Israel',[1] the true Israel is nevertheless to be found within the nominal Israel. Also, since only the Lord Himself knows who are truly His, men must often rightly and understandably treat the whole as if they were all genuine in order to allow the genuine thus to enjoy distinctive Christian ministry and to engage together in distinctive Christian worship and fellowship.

This does not mean, however, that in the Epistles no distinctions are made between professing Christians. Let us in illustration of this point consider St. Paul's Epistles to the Corinthians, particularly as some contend that, in spite of all

[1] Rom. ix. 6

the unworthy features of their church life, the apostle still addressed them all as only true Christians can be addressed. In writing to them St. Paul makes this distinction, 'And I, brethren, could not speak unto you as unto spiritual, but as unto carnal, even as unto babes in Christ.'[1] Here *carnal* Christians are distinguished from *spiritual* ones. This description 'carnal' might refer to members 'according to the flesh', who have no spiritual interests because they are not born of the Spirit. Certainly St. Paul's second letter to the Corinthians implies that he did not presume that they were all genuine believers.[2] For, after expounding to them the character of the ministry of reconciliation to which he was called, and the message which he preached, urging sinners to accept Christ's substitutionary work, and be reconciled to God,[3] he makes a gospel appeal to his readers. 'We then, as workers together with him, beseech you also that ye receive not the grace of God in vain.'[4] And he enforces this by quoting words from the prophet Isaiah: 'Behold, now is the accepted time; behold, now is the day of salvation.'[5] Here St. Paul is obviously urging any of his readers who have never embraced God's saving grace in Christ, to close with the offer of salvation now.

Again, later in the same Epistle, he writes: 'Examine yourselves, whether ye be in the faith; prove your own selves.'[6] Plainly, therefore, St. Paul did not regard all the nominal members of the church in Corinth as necessarily genuine members of Christ. Indeed, his presumption was that probably some were not. This is still a healthy presumption. There are always need and place for occasional evangelistic appeals even to outwardly established church members and regular communicants. Nor are there lacking in the local churches of our day those who can testify that, after many years as active but purely nominal Christians, they were converted in response to such an evangelistic appeal and entered into new life in Christ.

[1] 1 Cor. iii. 1

[2] For evidence that 1 Corinthians does not wholly imply it either, see 1 Cor. x. 1-12 and the comment on it on pages 19f.

[3] See 2 Cor. v. 14-21

[4] 2 Cor. vi. 1

[5] 2 Cor. vi. 2; from Is. xlix. 8

[6] 2 Cor. xiii. 5

In his use of the description 'carnal', however, it seems more likely, in the context already referred to,[1] that St. Paul was referring to genuine Spirit-born believers in Christ, but to ones who were in an unsatisfactory spiritual state. They had spiritual life, but they were still virtual 'babes in Christ'. They had failed to grow up as Christians. Their active interests were carnal and not spiritual. The apostle makes the same distinction between two types of genuine Christians in his Epistle to the Romans when he writes:

> For they that are after the flesh do mind the things of the flesh; but they that are after the Spirit the things of the Spirit.[2]

Here the implied warning is against wasting the earthly possibilities of one's life as a true Christian through letting one's life be dominated and determined by wrong interests, by the things of this world instead of the things of God. Such have, as St. Paul implies in the context where he refers to them, no appetite for, and no ability to digest, more solid spiritual food.

If we now return to the teaching of our Lord Himself we may find that in His very familiar parable of the sower, after referring to those who made no response to the word preached, He made similar distinction between three kinds of participants in the visible Church—between what we may call the 'carnal but merely nominal', who has no life in the Spirit, the 'genuine but carnal', whose life in the Spirit is starved and frustrated by improper interests, and the 'genuine and spiritual', the spiritually fruitful believer. For three kinds of visible growth followed the sowing of the seed of the word of God. These all represent additions to the visible community, or professing Church. Let us consider them one at a time.

The growth 'on the rock'[3] illustrates those who make no real heart response. Their self-will is not broken. There is no regenerating work of God deep within. Because their response is natural or 'according to the flesh' it is all outward and visible. Such apparent converts to Christ and His truth may thus temporarily make an impressive, open display of the new

[1] See 1 Cor. iii. 1 [2] Rom. viii. 5 [3] See Lk. viii. 6, 13

direction of their interest and activity both in word and deed. But they are not living members of Christ. 'These', Jesus said, 'have no root, which for a while believe, and in time of temptation fall away.'[1] Their professed faith, therefore, cannot have been real saving faith. Their temporary membership in the visible Church, no matter how active, is wholly nominal, not genuine. For had God begun a work in them by His Spirit, He would have completed it.[2] They would have endured to the end. It is against being fascinated and deceived by this type of 'convert' that some who are keen on evangelism particularly need to be beware. For true response proves its genuineness by endurance and ultimate fruitfulness. It is not best measured in terms of quick visible display.

The growth 'among thorns'[3] illustrates those who do embrace and possess deep within the gift of new life from God. Their response is not merely nominal and superficial; it is genuine. But its fruitfulness is frustrated by carnal and worldly interests, appetites and concerns. They are, said Jesus, 'choked with cares and riches and pleasures of this life, and bring no fruit to perfection'.[4]

The growth 'on the good ground' represents those who 'in an honest and good heart, having heard the word, keep it, and bring forth fruit with patience'.[5]

While some distinction between these three types may ultimately be made on earth and by men, either because of the failure of the supposed new life to survive, or because of the absence or presence in the life of the fruits of the Spirit, final distinction between them will be made by the Lord Himself and by His angels in the coming day of manifestation and of judgment. Then the purely nominal will be cast out, like the would-be guest at the wedding feast who had not on a wedding garment;[6] or they will be seen to have no enduring claim to belong at all. Then the carnal Christians, who have found new life in Christ, but who subsequently have wasted their earthly lives as Christians, will (to adapt phraseology of

[1] Lk. viii. 13
[2] See Phil. i. 6; 1 Thes. v. 23, 24
[3] See Lk. viii. 7, 14
[4] Lk. viii. 14
[5] Lk. viii. 8, 15
[6] See Mt. xxii. 11–14

St. Paul's) 'suffer loss', but they themselves 'shall be saved; yet so as through fire'.[1] Then the wholeheartedly spiritual Christians, who have grown on earth to maturity of Christian character, and have been made fruitful for God in life and service, will receive reward—the reward of appointment to do larger heavenly service, for which by such growth and experience they will obviously be qualified.[2]

Because of the solemn difference between these last two types of genuine Christians, the New Testament Epistles are particularly full of teaching and exhortation to Christians. They urge them to give their minds to spiritual things, fully to put on Christ, to grow up in understanding, to become active in good works, to be faithful in witness for Christ even unto death, so as to lay up treasure in heaven, and not to be disapproved and ashamed before Christ at His coming.

In the teaching of our Lord Himself, however, the most solemn and explicit emphasis is put on the inevitable ultimate separation between the merely nominal and the truly genuine, who temporarily appear united and to all outward appearance the same in the visible earthly community of His professed followers. Let us consider, in illustration of this, our Lord's parable of the ten virgins.[3] This is a parable of the visible professing Church, particularly of the single local congregation.

These ten virgins possessed many characteristics in common, which both distinguished them from others, and united them as a group. They had an openly-professed relation to the bridegroom. It was his person, and the prospect of his coming, that brought them together in this special way. Their virginity may, in the light of scriptural usage, be interpreted symbolically and morally, as suggesting freedom from spiritual fornication. They were none of them given to idolatry or to other gods. Their lamp-bearing and their forward-looking expectation may be taken to suggest the open profession of a calling yet to find its fulfilment when the bridegroom comes and the

[1] See 1 Cor. iii. 15, RV [2] See e.g. Mt. xxv. 14–30; Lk. xix. 11–27
[3] See Mt. xxv. 1–13

world's night is followed by the bridegroom's day. The intervening sleep, common to them all, may suggest the sleep of death, which intervenes before the great awakening and the final crisis. Then the wise are distinguished from the foolish by their possession or lack of something external to themselves received from another, namely oil to make their lamps burn—a picture surely of the regenerating and sanctifying Spirit, the source of true life within and of true light without. What was enough to keep the foolish within the visible community before the bridegroom came is not adequate to find acceptance in His presence when He comes. The foolish are not only shut out but also disowned. When they come to the door, already shut, and cry 'Lord, Lord, open to us', it is the bridegroom himself who answers, 'Verily I say unto you, I know you not.'

As the Lord Himself will thus eventually make all too plain, there is, therefore, a radical difference within the professing visible Church on earth between the genuine and the nominal members. Some are wise, and some are foolish.

This difference within a Christian congregation is sometimes made in measure apparent by the challenge of a preacher who calls church members to those very activities which the nominal members neglect, only to find some of them deliberately unwilling to engage in them. This kind of division happened, for example, among the Jews at the preaching of John the Baptist.[1]

When members of the one visible Church, particularly members of the same local congregation, are thus made aware, by the working of God's Spirit among them, that they are divided, that some delight in what others have no desire for, that some welcome as fundamental what others regard as unnecessary and out of place, what then is to be the relation of these two groups to one another? Should their unity be preserved? and if so, how? Or is either of the groups justified in beginning to function separately? These are some of the questions obviously to be faced in our next chapter.

[1] Lk. vii. 29, 30; cf. Mt. xxi. 28–32

CHAPTER TEN

FELLOWSHIP AND THE LOCAL CHURCHES

As we have noticed on more than one occasion already, individuals who by the Spirit, and through faith, respond to the call of God in Christ, are intended by God to find and to fulfil their vocation together. As St. Paul pertinently said to the Christians in Corinth when they were grievously divided:

> God is faithful, through whom ye were called into the fellowship of his Son Jesus Christ our Lord.[1]

This idea of fellowship in Christ, first with God and then with our fellow-believers, dominates the whole New Testament. So, for instance, St. John writes:

> That which we have seen and heard declare we unto you, that ye also may have fellowship with us: and truly our fellowship is with the Father, and with his Son Jesus Christ.
> If we say that we have fellowship with him, and walk in darkness, we lie, and do not the truth: but if we walk in the light, as he is in the light, we have fellowship one with another, and the blood of Jesus Christ his Son cleanseth us from all sin.[2]

Writing of the early days of the Church, Luke records how

> they continued stedfastly in . . . fellowship.[3] And the Lord added to them (mg. 'together') day by day those that were being saved.[4]

Any idea, therefore, of enjoying salvation or being a Christian in isolation is foreign to the New Testament writings.

In his Epistle to the Ephesians St. Paul uses three metaphors to describe the Church of Christ, the metaphors of a body,[5] a

[1] I Cor. i. 9, RV [2] I Jn. i. 3, 6, 7 [3] Acts ii. 42
[4] Acts ii. 47, RV [5] Eph. i. 22, 23, iv. 12–16

building[1] and a bride.[2] In the first place all three of these metaphors stress the decisive and distinctive relation of the Church as a whole, and of every individual in it, to the one Lord. Every member or stone finds his place, and the whole community fulfils its destiny, in vital fellowship with Christ as 'the head' of the body, 'the chief corner stone' of the building, and 'the husband' of the bride. In addition, the first two metaphors, of the body and of the building, also emphasize how this common relation to Christ involves all the members in a unity with one another, and in an interdependence upon one another.

After a recent careful examination in detail of the Pauline usage of these metaphors, Dr. Ernest Best concludes: 'Throughout all the metaphors it is consequently the internal relationship of Christ to the Church, and the mutual relationships of members to one another that is emphasized.'[3] Similarly of the use of the concept of 'the body of Christ' in St. Paul's earlier Epistles he also writes: 'The metaphor looks inward and not outward; it is used, not to express a truth about the place of the Church in the world, but about the relationships of members of the Church to Christ and to one another. . . . Thus in calling them members of the Body Paul seeks to teach their relationship and duties, not to the world, but to one another.'[4] For instance, what St. Paul himself says is: 'And the eye cannot say unto the hand, I have no need of thee: nor again the head to the feet, I have no need of you.'[5] And he adds that God's purpose in this arrangement is 'that the members should have the same care one for another'.[6] So, just as in the human body different members do different things, it is God's purpose that in the Church, by their faithful discharge of their different particular functions, the individual members should serve one another.

Nor is the particular place and function of each in relation to the rest self-chosen or man-determined. It is divinely-appointed and directly God-given. So St. Paul writes:

[1] Eph. ii. 20–22 [2] Eph. v. 25–32
[3] *One Body in Christ*, S.P.C.K., 1955, p. 189
[4] *Op. cit.*, p. 113 [5] 1 Cor. xii. 21 [6] 1 Cor. xii. 25

> For to one is given by the Spirit the word of wisdom; to another the word of knowledge by the same Spirit; to another faith by the same Spirit; to another the gifts of healing by the same Spirit; . . . but all these worketh that one and the selfsame Spirit, dividing to every man severally as he will.[1]

And later in the same passage, speaking metaphorically, he adds, 'But now hath God set the members every one of them in the body, as it hath pleased him'.[2]

This means, therefore, that as Christians we can be kept fully fit and grow to maturity, and fulfil our divinely-intended service, only by active co-operation with our fellow Christians. Every member of Christ's body the Church has his proper and necessary contribution to make to the well-being of the whole. None can be depised or disregarded, or for any other reason fail to function, without damage and loss to the body corporate.[3] Also, while some functions may seem more important or gain more prominence in the eyes of men, all are necessary. Nor are some less directly in touch with Christ than others, and so more dependent on some of their fellow Christians than on Christ Himself.

On this last point Dr. Ernest Best concludes, 'There is no suggestion that those with different functions stand in a different relationship to Christ.'[4] This is an important truth, because it denies in principle the idea prevalent in some quarters that the Church consists of a ministering clergy or hierarchy and a dependent laity. For while Christians do in measure all depend upon one another, they all primarily depend upon the living Christ Himself, and draw life and grace directly from Him through faith alone.[5] He is the one 'high priest over the house of God'. Also, they all enjoy, as priests, equal and full access to God in Christ.[6] So there is in the Church of Christ no priesthood limited, as in the old Israel, to a select class. The priesthood is a priesthood of all believers.[7]

[1] 1 Cor. xii. 8, 9, 11
[2] 1 Cor. xii. 18
[3] See 1 Cor. xii. 12–31; Rom. xii. 3–10
[4] *Op. cit.*, p. 188
[5] See Col. ii. 9
[6] See Heb. x. 19–22; 1 Tim. ii. 5
[7] See 1 Pet. ii. 5, 9

By thus realizing fellowship in Christ with one another, and functioning together for their mutual profit, and for the furtherance of God's will, Christians are intended by God to exhibit for His glory a supernatural and a super-national unity. Men and woman previously estranged from one another by all kinds of barriers of race, class, culture and religion are called by grace to experience and to practise fellowship as brethren in Christ. So St. Paul writes to Christians and says:

> Ye are all one in Christ Jesus.[1]
> Where there is neither Greek nor Jew, circumcision nor uncircumcision, Barbarian, Scythian, bond nor free: but Christ is all, and in all.[2]

This, indeed, is Christ's great distinctive work in a universe distracted and divided by evil, namely, by the miracle of divine redemption and re-creation, to rescue and to weld together into a living unity the broken and mutually hostile sections of sinful humanity:

> to make in himself of twain one new man, so making peace; and that he might reconcile both unto God in one body by the cross, having slain the enmity thereby.[3]

This miraculous company of the redeemed, thus reconciled to God and to one another, provides a pattern and a pledge of God's ultimate purpose for the whole universe, namely,

> that in the dispensation of the fulness of times he might gather together in one all things in Christ.[4]

So it is 'by the church' that even 'the principalities and powers in heavenly places' are learning more about the variegated wealth of the divine wisdom.[5]

Also, this unity, when thus realized in Christ by the Spirit, can be here and now such a witness to the world of the presence and power of God at work, that it will move men to accept the doctrine concerning the activity of God in Christ in saving grace that has brought it to pass. Thus our Lord's own prayer is answered—the prayer that His own may be one, and that the onlooking world, through seeing it, will believe

[1] Gal. iii. 28 [2] Col. iii. 11 [3] See Eph. ii. 13–18
[4] Eph. i. 10; cf. Col. i. 18–20 [5] See Eph. iii. 10

that out of love for men God the Father did send His own Son into the world to redeem them from their separation both from God and from one another, and to make possible such a consummation of realized fellowship with God and among men.[1]

Since all true believers in Christ, who are born of God's Spirit, are brought by divine grace into God's family, and are given 'the right to become children of God',[2] it is important that they should not only recognize, but also actively express, their new relationship to each other as brethren. So, in the New Testament Epistles, great attention is given to the way in which Christians act towards one another. Exhortations to pray for others are in the first place exhortations to pray for fellow-Christians. This is an activity in which the apostle Paul continually engaged;[3] and so he writes to tell Christians that they should be 'praying always with all prayer and supplication in the Spirit, . . . for all saints'.[4] Similarly, exhortations to show active love, and to engage in deeds of kindness, towards all men, including enemies, are specially and most of all exhortations thus to serve one's brethren in Christ. So, again, St. Paul writes to Christians:

> Bear ye one another's burdens, and so fulfil the law of Christ . . . As we have therefore opportunity, let us do good unto all men, especially unto them who are of the household of faith.[5]

Indeed, did not our Lord Himself say 'by this shall all men know that ye are my disciples, if ye have love one to another'?[6]

In the New Testament Epistles it is also assumed that Christians living in the same place will have constant intercourse among themselves and will meet regularly together as one body. So, for instance, in writing his letters to the Christians in Corinth St. Paul addressed himself to 'the church of God which is at Corinth'.[7] Also, in more than one section of the first Epistle, the apostle refers to ways of behaviour 'in the church',[8] that is, in the congregation, when, as he says,

[1] See Jn. xvii. 20–23 [2] Jn. i. 12, RV [3] See Rom. i. 9; Col. i. 9, etc.
[4] Eph. vi. 18 [5] Gal. vi. 2, 10 [6] Jn. xiii. 35
[7] 1 Cor. i. 2; 2 Cor. i. 1 [8] See 1 Cor. xiv. 19, 28, 35

'the whole church be come together into one place'.[1] By so doing Christians make their prayers corporate,[2] and their worship of God public. It is, too, at such times that some gifts of the Spirit can best be exercised in ministry to the brethren;[3] and only through such active and regular membership in the congregation can individual believers gain necessary teaching and pastoral care. When Christians thus assemble themselves together is also the appropriate time 'to eat the Lord's supper',[4] in obedience to the Lord's own command, and in remembrance of Him and of His atoning death for us sinners. No Christian, therefore, can get from, or give to, both the Lord and his fellow-Christians all that he ought, unless he regularly joins actively in meetings of Christians in his locality.

By thus establishing a regular, public meeting of Christians, that is, a local church, there is provided a pillar and a buttress for the truth.[5] In other words, witness for Christ and the gospel in that place is given greater public prominence and more enduring permanence. Also, Christians should thus together visibly constitute a colony of heaven,[6] and by their actions, both among themselves, and in relation to the world in which they sojourn, should make onlookers aware of the distinctive standards of the heavenly city to which they belong.

Our Lord Himself taught that a company of Christians meeting together in His name, and as the local church, may expect to enjoy blessings not possible in the same way to isolated individuals. He said that they may expect a special experience of His own manifested presence—'there am I in the midst of them'. He said that to them would be given increased confidence and assurance in making requests in prayer:

> That if two of you shall agree on earth as touching any thing that they shall ask, it shall be done for them of my Father which is in heaven.

He said that they would be enabled to reach decisively binding agreement in moral judgment on matters of practical concern

[1] I Cor. xiv. 23 [2] E.g. Acts xii. 5 [3] See I Cor. xii. 28
[4] See I Cor. xi. 20–34 [5] See I Tim. iii. 15 [6] See Phil. iii. 20

to the brethren—'Whatsoever ye shall bind on earth shall be bound in heaven.'[1]

What is also noteworthy here is the explicit place given by our Lord to 'two or three'.[2] He thereby encouraged small informal meetings, and implied that, in principle, such a gathering would be a true church meeting, with the supreme decisive sanction of His own presence in the midst. Similarly in the Epistles exhortations are given which can only fully be acted on by small groups functioning in intimate fellowship. For Christians are told to 'exhort one another'[3]—not always to sit and listen while the same person does all the speaking to a large silent congregation. A number of Christians are exhorted to act together in order to help any single one of their number who is in danger of falling by the way.[4] One thinks, for example, of the way in which some mountain climbing is undertaken, by a small team roped together. This method enables the others unitedly to help the one who may be in difficulties or facing danger. Such fellowship can be fully entered into only in a small team. John Wesley broke congregations up into class meetings which were small enough for every member to count and to become vocal. When the writer to the Hebrews says in exhortation, 'Not forsaking the assembling of ourselves together', it is possible that he means, Let us not give up our additional small meeting because such an occasion can be used to great profit in mutual provocation and encouragement.[5]

In the realm of sport many enthusiastic supporters of local football or cricket teams, who are always in their seats to watch the game when there is a home match, and are sometimes good critics of the play, are spectators only. They do not themselves play the game. They could not be called on to fill a place in the team. Much of our local church life, particularly when the congregation is large, is similarly weak. The majority are, for the most part, silent listeners and interested onlookers.

[1] See Mt. xviii. 15–20 [2] Mt. xviii. 16, 20 [3] Heb. iii. 13, x. 25
[4] See Gal. vi. 1; Heb. iii. 12, 13 [5] See Heb. x. 24, 25

They are not all active participants in giving ministry as well as receiving it. So, neither they, nor the vitality and fruitfulness of the congregation, make much progress.

Such church members need to learn to open their mouths in prayer, and in exposition and exhortation based on the written Word of God, by meeting informally with one or two others to pray and to study together the Bible, and to find, as they do so, that, true to His promise, Christ Himself is in their midst. Also, they would do well to remember that, in addition to the chosen twelve,

> the Lord appointed other seventy also, and sent them two and two before his face into every city and place, whither he himself would come.[1]

Such activity should be encouraged more officially by congregations and their ministers, and both reckoned, and proved to be, a vital expression of true fellowship in Christ.

Nor can we avoid facing the fact that in a local congregation spiritual activities properly distinctive of true Christians may themselves prove divisive. For instance, in his first letter to the Corinthians, in addition to rebuking them for their unchristian divisions and exhorting them to be united,[2] Paul refers later[3] to the report that had reached him that proper participation together in the Lord's supper was being prevented by the unworthy behaviour of some. 'When ye come together in the church,' he writes, 'I hear that divisions (or schisms) exist among you.' Here he does not say that such divisions are wholly wrong, but rather that they are inevitable. 'For there must be also heresies (or factions) among you,' he adds, 'that they which are approved may be made manifest among you.' In other words, actual participation together in distinctive Christian activity, or the challenge to do so, must sooner or later reveal in a congregation which members are 'spiritual' and which are 'carnal'. For, as we saw in the previous chapter, the visible church is commonly divided into three or four characteristic types. Because these divisions are radical, they

[1] Lk. x. 1 [2] 1 Cor. i. 10–13 [3] 1 Cor. xi. 17–22, RV and mg.

are bound at times openly to appear. For instance, they commonly do appear in connection with the character and choice of interests to which members of a congregation may wish to give themselves in their weekday activities together. To be specific: should these be predominantly social, cultural and entertaining? or should they be spiritual, self-denying, and truly edifying? Should the church run whist drives, or dramatics, and allow dancing? Or should it concentrate on Bible study, prayer meetings, doctrinal and ethical teaching and discussion, active evangelism and practical ministry to those in need?

Let us, in illustration, quote from the apostle Paul himself. Writing to the Galatians, he says:

> Brethren, if a man be overtaken in a fault, ye which are spiritual, restore such an one in the spirit of meekness.[1]

Here he recognizes that some of his readers have a sensitiveness and a spiritual capacity not possessed by the rest, which qualify them for needed ministry to individuals beset and ensnared by temptation and sin. So he urges them as a group to function together in this way.

Similarly, writing to the Corinthians, he says first, 'Howbeit we speak wisdom among the perfect', or 'full-grown', or 'mature'. 'But he that is spiritual judgeth all things.'[2] Then he adds, 'And I, brethren, could not speak unto you as unto spiritual, but as unto carnal, even as unto babes in Christ.'[3] Here there is a pointed distinction in capacity and in appetite between two types of Christians, between the 'spiritual' and 'full-grown', on the one hand, and the 'carnal' and 'babes' on the other. When these two types exist side by side, as they often do, in the same congregation, it is to be expected that the spiritual will desire, and be capable of, activities and ministries, in which the carnal will have little or no interest, and no ability to participate.

What is more, when those truly born of the Spirit thus give expression to their new spiritual interests and capacities within a congregation, the probability is that they will be actively

[1] Gal. vi. 1 [2] 1 Cor. ii. 6, 15, RV and mg. [3] 1 Cor. iii. 1

opposed, and even deliberately frustrated, by that section of the congregation which consists of members who are merely nominal. For if the genuine but carnal church members fail to support spiritual activities because of their absorption in other interests, the merely nominal and wholly carnal church members, who are not born of the Spirit at all, are bound to oppose such activity. Not only have they no capacity to share in it, not only is its introduction an embarrassment to them, but the suggestion that participation in it is a mark of genuineness is a direct reflection on their own spiritual state, and implies that their own participation in church ceremonies and services is not enough to secure a place in the family of God.

So, says St. Paul, with Ishmael's mocking of Isaac in the household of Abraham in mind, 'But as then he that was born after the flesh persecuted him that was born after the Spirit, even so it is now'.[1] Commenting on this statement Martin Luther wrote: 'Whosoever are born and live in Christ, and rejoice in this birth and inheritance of God, have Ishmael for their enemy and their persecutor.' 'This persecution always remains in the church, especially when the doctrine of the gospel flourisheth, to wit, that the children of the flesh mock the children of the promise, and persecute them.'[2]

This Old Testament illustration from the circumcised household of Abraham itself suggests that this kind of persecution of the genuine by the nominal members is particularly likely to arise in a visible baptized congregation, which has been largely nominal in its membership, or even spiritually 'dead',[3] like the church in Sardis; but in whose midst a work of God results in some being born of God's Spirit. So the new converts or true 'believers' find that those who ought to be their elder brethren to encourage them in their new-found life in Christ are those who most oppose their desire to pursue such spiritual interests, particularly at times by their mockery.

The practical question then arises, What are the genuinely spiritual to do in such circumstances? For the congregation to

[1] Gal. iv. 29 [2] Commentary on Galatians, *in loc.* [3] Rev. iii. 1

which they belong is the visible professing church of God in that place. Their own presence in it is proof that the Spirit of God has not ceased to be active among its members. Nor is it possible to hive off in order to form a new congregation, which will be one hundred per cent perfect. For no earthly congregation is, or can be, this. In addition, there are probably others in the congregation, who, like the seven thousand in Israel who were unknown to Elijah, are true children of God as yet unknown to them. They ought not to forsake these, but rather to seek to find them and to have spiritual fellowship with them. Also, they should prayerfully seek within the congregation, by their good works rather than by offensively preaching at others, to let their light shine. For God uses such a witness to cause some who see it to glorify Him.[1]

But, on the other hand, it is surely right that such a group of spiritually-minded Christians should now engage together in the kind of spiritual activities needful for their well-being and fruitfulness. And, if the congregation and its minister will not officially sponsor such activities in connection with the church, it cannot be wrong for them to meet together in Christ's name to further these ends. Only if they do so, indeed, will they be able fully to glorify God within the congregation as well as in the outside world. If, in the end, they are virtually pushed out, as both our Lord and St. Paul were forced to cease from synagogue attendance, and are thus compelled to start independent meetings, then there is good precedent for departing. Also, they can find in the Scriptures ground for the confidence that, when the Lord comes Himself to separate the nominal from the genuine, the tables will be turned. It is those 'born after the flesh' who will then be 'cast out'.[2]

What is plainly normal, however, according to the New Testament, is for the individual Christian to be enjoying regular, active fellowship with fellow-Christians, and to find this fellowship in the local church particularly on the Lord's day.[3] Ideally such a congregation should be a mixture of all

[1] See Mt. v. 10–12, 15, 16 [2] See Gal. iv. 30

[3] See Acts xx. 7; 1 Cor. xvi. 2; Rev. i. 10

ages, and varied types, of both sexes. It should have more mature members, able, as we shall consider in the next chapter, to shoulder responsibility, as the Lord may call and equip, for spiritual oversight, pastoral care, systematic teaching, and scriptural exhortation and admonition. It is inadequate, and can prove unhealthy, for Christians permanently to make a special organization, limited in membership to one type, sex or age-group, their main sphere of Christian fellowship. While such fellowships can have some value as an extra to congregational worship, or some place in special circumstances (for instance, where students are temporarily thrown together during a college course), participation in it is no proper equivalent to active membership in a local church. Particularly is it true that young Christians need the guidance, discipline, and understanding of all that is involved in Christian living which come from fellowship with, and proper subjection to, older Christians. They ought not to treat their Young People's Fellowship as more important than the local congregation, and, of course, wiser than the minister, the church council, or the deacons' meeting! So St. Peter says:

> Ye younger, submit yourselves unto the elder, Yea, all of you be subject one to another, and be clothed with humility: for God resisteth the proud, and giveth grace to the humble.[1]

An important test of the character and grounds of Christian fellowship is provided by the case of an individual Christian moving from one place to take up residence in another. Surely what he ought to find is that the new congregation to which he goes will welcome him as a brother in the Lord because he belongs to Christ. The same confession of faith in Jesus as Lord, which led possibly to his baptism, and certainly to his acceptance into full membership in the congregation which he has left, ought to be the sufficient ground of his welcome in the congregation to which he comes.

Yet experience shows that often more attention is paid to the character of the congregation, of which the man was previously a member, than to the fundamental question

[1] 1 Pet. v. 5

whether he is one of Christ's people or not. So-called proper church membership, judged, that is, by some one particular denominational standard, is treated at times as more important and decisive than personal relation to the one Lord. The guidance which St. Paul gives to Christians who may differ in practice on matters of religious observance or conscientious scruple is not to make a man's attitude on such doubtful questions the decisive test of his reception or rejection as a Christian; but to receive as brethren all those whom it is plain God and Christ have already received.[1]

This simple principle and proper Christian priority may also help us to arrive at a positive attitude on the confused and difficult problem, as many have made it to be, of the interrelation of the local churches. Local churches, like individual Christians, ought to be able to recognize one another as Christian and to join in active fellowship by direct reference to their common Lord, without any overriding reference to some human third party, or to some limiting denominational requirement. This will surely mean, for instance, that their members can unite in occasional participation together in the Lord's supper. If their forms of worship and their church order are different, they may not be able so readily to unite and co-operate in every activity or church action, any more than Christians who speak different languages can do so, but they will be made conscious that their unity in Christ is primary, and their differences of expression and practice secondary, and often complementary.

It is important also to remember and to rejoice in the liberty of the Spirit which is given to all who are in Christ. Our Lord and the New Testament writers give no rigid organizational instructions. Within loyalty to the one Lord, and to the truth revealed in Him and in His Word, there is scope for great variety. The right principle, for instance, of episcopal oversight in the congregation may find varying expressions in bishops, presbyters, or pastors. The distinctiveness and the unity of the Christian Church is that of a flock, united by

[1] See Rom. xiv. 1–3, xv. 7

every individual's attachment to the one Shepherd. It is no longer, as Jewish separateness and solidarity were, that of a fold, in which members are penned together, and separated from others, by elaborate outward forms. It is absurd, therefore, that sectional attachment to certain forms, whether of church order or of congregational worship, should prevent those who are brethren in Christ from openly recognizing and expressing their brotherly relationship to one another.

In this connection it is plain for all to see that the wider grouping into artificial denominations of local congregations, which happen to prefer (or more often simply to have inherited) their own distinctive form of church order or government, only helps to prevent geographically adjacent Christian congregations from coming into closer fellowship. In such a situation the more distant denominational loyalty is sometimes painfully formal, unreal and fettering, and more binding financially than spiritually. Nor can this frustration of local fellowship be rightly relieved by increased bureaucratic control at some earthly centre. Rather ought such separated local congregations to realize closer fellowship together by looking direct to their common spiritual Head, and coming together in Him.

Yet there must surely be some necessary safeguard and standard, to preserve and inform such fellowship, and to prevent it from becoming just natural and social, and ceasing or failing to be truly spiritual and Christian. This clearly is where truth divinely revealed is so important and so decisive. What makes the Christian community unique and different from all others, and what ought to secure its unity in action as well as in confession, is positive loyalty to the truth as it is in Jesus,[1] truth in which every true Christian is given understanding by the indwelling Spirit,[2] truth which is to be discerned through the divinely-inspired Word.[3] This, then, is where acknowledgement of the supreme authority of the Old and New Testament Scriptures, and sincere agreement

[1] See Eph. iv. 20, 21
[2] See 1 Jn. ii. 20, 27; 1 Cor. ii. 9–12
[3] See Jn. viii. 31, 32, xvii. 17

concerning scriptural teaching in matters both of faith and practice, are so indispensable and important.

A large orchestra and choir are able to realize elaborate harmony in performance, not when separate individuals or groups copy each other, but when each plays or sings his own distinctive part. What unites them all is their willing submission to the control of one conductor. What enables them to contribute varied parts harmoniously is obedience to the printed score, response to the conductor's guidance, and attentive awareness of the stage reached by the contributions of others. Somewhat similarly in his letter to the Ephesians, St. Paul, when he exhorts Christians to strive towards a mature and crowning expression of unity in Christ, indicates that this can be achieved only if they are sound in doctrine and sincere in practice.

On the one hand, he says, we must 'henceforth be no more children, tossed to and fro, and carried about with every wind of doctrine'. For we can 'come . . . unto a perfect man, unto the measure of the stature of the fulness of Christ', only in the unity of the faith, and of the knowledge of the Son of God.[1] On the other hand, we shall 'grow up into him in all things', and see His body truly increased and edified, only if we live 'the truth in love'.[2]

Finally, the great feast of fellowship with the Lord and with one another, the Lord's own supper, ought to be used by Christians more evangelically and less ecclesiastically than it often is. For it is the sacrament not of the Church, but of the Lord and of the gospel. Those who partake in it should be expressing not their membership in some particular church, but their common relation to the one Lord, and their reception, as repentant and believing sinners, of the benefits of His atoning death, which are offered to men in the gospel. This surely is the best place and way to deepen, and to express visibly, our spiritual oneness with one another.

> Seeing that there is one bread, we, who are many, are one body: for we all partake from the one bread.[3]

[1] See Eph. iv. 15, 16
[2] See Eph. iv. 13, 14
[3] Cor. x. 17. RV and mg.

CHAPTER ELEVEN

PASTORS AND TEACHERS

IN the full statement of His mind and will the risen Lord, prior to His ascension, gave to His followers a twofold task,—to preach and to teach. They were to win converts to Himself in repentance and faith and declared allegiance, and then to guide and instruct them in a new life of obedience. To quote His own words:

> Go ye therefore, and make disciples of all the nations, baptizing them into the name of the Father and of the Son and of the Holy Ghost: teaching them to observe all things whatsoever I commanded you.[1]

In His more personal commission to Simon Peter we find, too, that our Lord put special emphasis on ministry to his fellow disciples. When He warned Peter of impending danger, and predicted that he would thrice deny that he knew Him, Jesus also said:

> But I made supplication for thee, that thy faith fail not: and do thou, when once thou hast turned again, stablish thy brethren.[2]

After His resurrection, when our Lord talked intimately with Peter about his love and loyalty, three times He repeated similar injunctions, namely: 'Feed my lambs.' 'Feed my sheep.' 'Feed my sheep.'[3]

In addition, therefore, to evangelism in order to add disciples to the Christian community by preaching the gospel, there is need of teaching and pastoral care within the Church thus gathered, in order to make disciples aware of the Lord's own instructions, and to watch over them and to help them fully to live the life of obedience. So, in addition to 'apostles and prophets', who were, as we have seen, given by the Lord at the beginning to serve as the foundation of the Church,[4]

[1] Mt. xxviii. 19, 20, RV
[2] Lk. xxii. 32, RV
[3] Jn. xxi. 15–17
[4] See Eph. ii. 20

and in addition to 'evangelists', whose continuing ministry in the Church is of primary importance because through their ministry individuals are brought to a saving knowledge of Christ and by Him added to the Church, the ascended Lord has also given 'some, pastors and teachers; for the perfecting of the saints'.[1]

The New Testament records also indicate that this divine provision is directly given to, and intended to function in, the local churches. For instance we find that when, by the blessing of God, groups of disciples had been won to faith in Christ in three or four centres in South Galatia, Paul and Barnabas 'appointed for them elders in every church'.[2] Later we read of St. Paul sending from Miletus to Ephesus, and calling to him 'the elders of the church' there. In the course of his solemn charge to them, he said:

> Take heed unto yourselves, and to all the flock, in the which the Holy Ghost hath made you bishops (mg. 'overseers'), to feed the church of God, which he purchased with his own blood.[3]

This important verse reveals first, that one congregation had several 'elders' or 'presbyters' (Gk. *presbuteroi*); second, that the same men were also called 'bishops' or 'overseers';[4] third, that this ministry is no mere human idea, but a divine appointment—it was the Spirit who made them bishops; and fourth, that their work was to act as shepherds (Gk. *poimainein*) and to 'pastor' or 'feed' the Church of God.

This means, therefore, that in New Testament times the names 'elder' (or 'presbyter'), 'bishop', and 'pastor' (or 'shepherd') were alternative names for the same ministers. It also means that the proper sphere of such ministry is in one city or local church.[5] So that, in the local congregations of our own day, an anglican minister or 'priest' (a name which is etymologically and historically in this connection a shortened form of 'presbyter', and not the word for one who offers sacrifice), a presbyterian elder, and a baptist pastor, are all slightly varying forms of this proper local church ministry, which may in

[1] Eph. iv. 11, 12
[2] Acts xiv. 23, RV
[3] Acts xx. 28, RV
[4] Cf. Tit. i. 5–9
[5] See Tit. i. 5

character rightly be described as equally episcopal, presbyterian and pastoral. Such 'bishops', in this simple New Testament sense, are not essential to the existence and visible emergence of a local church, but they are (in the plural) an important part of its divinely-intended fullness, and generally necessary to its true well-being.

It is wrong, therefore, that Christian churches should be divided by their attachment to one or other of these varying forms of the same essential ministry; just as it was completely unchristian that the church in Corinth, to which St. Paul wrote, should be divided by its members' attachment to different ministers, one against another. In answer to this travesty of the truth St. Paul contends that salvation is found in Christ and Him crucified, and not in any minister; and that far from the churches or groups within them belonging to their ministers, the true ministers of God all belong equally to the church and to the people of God whom they are appointed to serve. So he writes:

> Now I beseech you, brethren, by the name of our Lord Jesus Christ, that ye all speak the same thing, and that there be no divisions among you; . . . For it hath been declared unto me of you, . . . that there are contentions among you. Now this I say, that every one of you saith, I am of Paul; and I of Apollos; and I of Cephas; and I of Christ. Is Christ divided? was Paul crucified for you? or were ye baptized in the name of Paul?[1]
> Therefore let no man glory in men. For all things are yours; whether Paul, or Apollos, or Cephas, . . . all are yours; and ye are Christ's; and Christ is God's.[2]

Nor is there any New Testament justification for confining ministry in the congregation to one man or to one class only. The church at Philippi, for instance, had several 'bishops' and also 'deacons'.[3] And, as we have seen already, the Lord by His Spirit gives to every member of His body a distinctive gift and ministry which ought to be exercised to God's glory and in the service of the brethren for the good of the whole body.[4] Also, since in Christ the whole laity is a priesthood, and every

[1] 1 Cor. i. 10–13
[2] 1 Cor. iii. 21–23
[3] Phil. i. 1
[4] See Rom. xii. 4–8

member has equal access to God, there are some ministries, like leading a congregation publicly to the throne of grace in prayer, which any member may fulfil.

Indeed, it is of decisive fundamental importance to remember that the Greek words *hiereis* and *hierateuma*, which describe priests who offer sacrifice, are never once in the New Testament used to describe the special ministers of the Church, such as the presbyters or bishops. But they are used to describe the general character both of the whole people of God in Christ, and of the divine service in which they are all alike called to share. For instance, St. Peter writes of all who are joined to Christ in saving faith: 'Ye are . . . an holy priesthood, to offer up spiritual sacrifices, acceptable to God by Jesus Christ.'[1] Similarly, in the Revelation of St. John we read of Christ that He 'hath made us kings and priests unto God and his Father'.[2] Also, because in our language the word 'priest', though etymologically derived from 'presbyter', is the only word we have to translate the Greek word *hiereus*, and to describe one who offers sacrifice, the use of the word 'priest' to describe a 'presbyter' (as in the Prayer Book of the Church of England) is theologically confusing. So clarity of understanding would be furthered, and closer scriptural fellowship with other Christians made more easy, if ministers who correspond in character to the New Testament 'presbyters' were never called 'priests', but were described either as 'elders' (as in AV, RV, and RSV) or as 'presbyters'—a translation significantly adopted even by the Roman Catholic Ronald A. Knox.

According to the New Testament witness, the elders who exercise oversight and minister the word in any local congregation should all be men. The public worship and prayer of the congregation should normally be led by men.[3] Nor should women teach men the things of God or bear rule over men.[4] But if it is done by them with due seemliness, it would appear from 1 Corinthians xi that women may lead in prayer or give an inspirational word in the congregation.[5] Their chief work, however, is obviously among women and children;

[1] 1 Pet. ii. 5, cf. verse 9 [2] Rev. i. 6, cf. v. 10 [3] 1 Tim. ii. 8
[4] 1 Tim. ii. 11, 12 [5] 1 Cor. xi. 5, 13

and in the discharge of those ministries particularly suited to women,[1] in the discharge of which they are divinely called to be true ministers or 'deaconesses'[2] of God and of the churches.

Here it is not unimportant to notice that in the New Testament the administration of baptism and of the Lord's supper is not restricted to one class of minister alone. If, as Church history has vindicated, any Christian may baptize another, it ought equally to be recognized, in principle, that, provided before God it is 'done decently and in order',[3] any Christian congregation may appoint any one of its number to administer the Lord's supper. It is absurd that congregations of true believers should be deprived for long periods of sharing in this ordinance because one particular type of minister is not available to them. On the other hand, if, as would appear, it is normally good that only elders or formally ordained ministers should exercise this responsibility, then each congregation ought to have a number of them.

If we are to be guided by the New Testament, it is also right to recognize that elders, or 'pastors and teachers', are given a position of special responsibility and importance. With reference to them St. Paul writes to Christians:

> And we beseech you, brethren, to know them which labour among you, and are over you in the Lord, and admonish you; and to esteem them very highly in love for their work's sake.[4] Let the elders that rule well be counted worthy of double honour, especially they who labour in the word and doctrine.[5]

This latter injunction obviously implies, in its context, that such ministers should be materially supported.[6] Such scriptural statements also indicate that the most important work that such elders do is by the ministry of the word of God[7] and by teaching. It would appear, in addition, that the phrase 'pastors and teachers' is not a reference to two different types of ministers, but rather a full indication of the two complementary types of ministry which elders in the local churches are appointed to fulfil. Only if they fulfil them will all the

[1] 1 Tim. v. 10 [2] Rom. xvi. 1, 2; see RV mg.
[3] 1 Cor. xiv. 40 [4] 1 Thes. v. 12, 13 [5] 1 Tim. v. 17
[6] See 1 Tim. v. 18; cf. Gal. vi. 6 [7] See Heb. xiii. 7

saints in any congregation be so qualified for their work of ministry that the whole body will be edified. Such seems to be the full significance of the context in which occurs the reference to the Lord's appointment of 'pastors and teachers'.[1]

This means also that the important succession to be preserved in any congregation in the interests of its own spiritual life and well-being is the faithful handing on of the deposit of revealed truth, 'the faith which once was for all delivered unto the saints',[2] which St. Paul called, in writing to Timothy, 'the form of sound words, which thou hast heard of me'.[3] What is desirable is that it should be taught afresh in the congregation to every new generation of hearers. So St. Paul enjoined Timothy:

> And the things that thou hast heard of me among many witnesses, the same commit thou to faithful men, who shall be able to teach others also.[4]

It is here in this sphere of ministry in the congregation that there are also great potential dangers, dangers of which there are many warnings in the Bible. In Old Testament times, for instance, none did more damage to the spiritual life of Israel than false prophets and corrupt priests; and the more so because a self-willed and indulgent people often welcomed such perverted leadership. So we find that from the first the apostle Paul had need to warn his converts against false teaching, and to urge them to exercise their own spiritual judgment to discern good from evil. 'Prove all things', he writes; 'hold fast that which is good.'[5]

Those who through the enlightenment of the Spirit have embraced the gospel of divine grace, and know Christ as Lord, should not be misled by teachers who claim ecclesiastical status of heavenly origin and yet deny revealed truth. So St. Paul writes:

> But though we, or an angel from heaven, preach any other gospel unto you than that which we have preached unto you, let him be accursed.[6]

[1] See Eph. iv. 11–13 [2] Jude 3, RV [3] 2 Tim. i. 13
[4] 2 Tim. ii. 2 [5] 1 Thes. v. 21 [6] Gal. i. 8

The need to heed this warning is the more urgent because such dangers to Christian faith and obedience may arise not only from without, but also from within the professing church and from among its accredited pastors and teachers. So, speaking to the elders of the church at Ephesus, St. Paul says:

> For I know this, that after my departing shall grievous wolves enter in among you, not sparing the flock. Also of your own selves shall men arise, speaking perverse things, to draw away disciples after them.[1]

Here the apostle finds hope of their preservation not in the bishops and their offices, but in the faithfulness of God, and in His gracious and authoritative Word. So St. Paul concludes:

> And now, brethren, I commend you to God, and to the word of his grace, which is able to build you up, and to give you an inheritance among all them which are sanctified.[2]

So those appointed to exercise rule or pastoral oversight in the churches should do so in submission to the God-given Word of truth, and by its faithful and diligent use in preaching and teaching, in exhortation and in admonition.[3]

In a situation like ours today, in which many Christian churches exist, and in which evangelistic missionary enterprise is widespread, local churches have to face the further question of forming a right attitude to Christian preachers and teachers, who come from elsewhere, and who may look to them for support in the work of evangelism, or for opportunity to engage among them in the ministry of teaching. Valuable guidance on these matters is to be found in two of the least read and least known Epistles of the New Testament, 2 and 3 John. Let us see what we can learn from them.

The second Epistle of John reveals the rise of false teachers, who affected superior knowledge. In their teaching they set a lead which left the teaching of Christ behind.[4] Their condemnation was that they 'confess not that Jesus Christ is come in the flesh. This', says John, 'is a deceiver and an antichrist'.[5] For

[1] Acts xx. 29, 30 [2] Acts xx. 32
[3] See 1 Tim. iv. 13; 2 Tim. iii. 14–iv. 5 [4] See 2 Jn. 9 [5] 2 Jn. 7

what claimed to be progress was fatal error. So the Christians of the local church to which St. John writes are told by the apostle to investigate the credentials of any would-be teacher who comes to them from elsewhere. The decisive test is not what local church he belongs to, nor what personal commission or ordination he may claim to possess, but what teaching he brings, and what doctrine he confesses. If he does not positively confess and teach the truth as they know it in Christ, he is neither to be received by them as a teacher, nor recommended as such to other churches.[1]

What is significant here is that the church members are told to judge for themselves, and on doctrinal grounds. They have every right to ask the would-be teacher to confess the true faith before they welcome him. It is, therefore, clearly appropriate for Christian congregations to ask possible ministers of the Word, whom they might like to welcome but who are unknown to them, to confirm their orthodoxy by a fresh personal confession of the faith. In the sixteenth and seventeenth centuries the Reformers made much of this principle. Before men were given freedom to minister in churches they had afresh to assent in full detail to a confession of the faith. There is still need for a continuance of this practice.

The third Epistle of John brings to our notice a ruling elder in a local church who is making excessive and improper claims to authority, and using his authority to refuse fellowship and help to missionaries of the gospel who happened to visit the place where he was, on their way to the people whom they hoped to evangelize. He not only refuses to welcome them to the local church, but forbids church members to have fellowship with them, and threatens to excommunicate any who do. His very words are malicious.[2]

In the face of such a situation the apostle John by-passes the ruling elder, and writes to a church member of spiritual quality, who, John hears, has been engaging in this forbidden activity, in order to commend him, and to encourage him to continue. John declares that such active fellowship with self-

[1] 2 Jn. 10

[2] See 3 Jn. 9, 10

sacrificing servants of God is worthy of God Himself, and makes those who offer it true fellow-helpers in the propagation of the gospel in the world.[1] Nor are the issues thus dealt with in this Epistle no longer relevant to local church life in our own day. There are ruling elders still who try to forbid active fellowship and co-operation between genuine Christians whose sole concern in such fellowship is the furtherance of the gospel. Such Christians, when thus opposed and 'forbidden', may find in this Epistle needed encouragement not to be overawed by the pretentious claims of men, but fearlessly to show fellowship in a way worthy of God and of His family to which they belong.

To the present writer, at least, if not to all Christians, it also seems right to recognize that in the parables of the mustard seed and of the leaven, particularly in the context in which they are to be found in the Gospel according to St. Matthew, our Lord Himself gave similar warning about the inevitable dangers, to the work of His kingdom, of wrong teaching and of improper hierarchical ambition and domination.[2]

Many scholars have recognized that, in the section of the first Gospel in which the series of seven parables of the kingdom occurs, the record as a whole reveals our Lord both acknowledging, and preparing His followers to face, some of the unexpected and outwardly disappointing features that must attend the fulfilment of God's purposes in the world. For He knew that the Jewish religious leaders had decisively rejected His claims.[3] He knew that the signs of His divine origin and mission, afforded by His miracles, had not brought about repentance on the part of the common people.[4] He knew that the last state of 'this wicked generation' would be worse than the first.[5] But He also was sure that the purposes of God

[1] See 3 Jn. 5–8

[2] The interpretation here offered is to be found in expanded form in *The Parables of the Kingdom*, by G. Campbell Morgan, Hodder & Stoughton, 1907

[3] See Mt. xii. 1–42, especially 10, 14, 24, 31, 34

[4] See Mt. xi. 20–24

[5] See Mt. xii. 43–45

were not being frustrated; and that there were those who, with Him, would find their delight in doing God's will.[1] So we read:

> At that time Jesus answered and said, I thank thee, O Father, Lord of heaven and earth, because thou hast hid these things from the wise and prudent, and hast revealed them unto babes. Even so, Father: for so it seemed good in thy sight.[2]

It seems appropriate, therefore, to recognize in the series of parables teaching corresponding to this situation. This is exactly what we find in the first two parables, the parable of the sower, and the parable of the wheat and the tares. The first of these suggests that there would be deep, enduring, fruitful response to our Lord's preaching from at the most a quarter of His hearers; and that much of the professed response would prove either completely superficial or grievously half-hearted.[3] The second parable foretells that where healthy and promising growth does take place there will be active opposition and counterfeit of a subtle and a confusing kind, resulting in the production of a mixture of good and bad, which must be allowed to continue until the end of the world.[4]

In our Lord's parable of the mustard seed,[5] therefore, may not the growth of a herb or plant into a tree be intended to suggest unnatural development, an attempt to become something never intended? Nor may it be without some relevance that in the Old Testament a tree is used figuratively to denote worldly empire and political greatness;[6] and that, in our Lord's previous parable of the sower, 'the birds of the air' represent agents of evil.

Is not the true work of God in the world done in quiet and unobtrusive ways, by the lowly rather than by the pretentious? Is there not some justification from history itself for thinking that the Church of God becomes perverted in character and interest when she tries to copy the forms and methods of the kingdoms of this world? Does not such development invite many from outside, who have no spiritual life or interest, to look to the Church simply for worldly shelter and material

[1] See Mt. xii. 46–50 [2] Mt. xi. 25, 26 [3] See Mt. xiii. 3–9, 18–23
[4] See Mt. xiii. 24–30, 36–43
[5] See Mt. xiii. 31, 32; cf. Lk. xiii. 18, 19 [6] See Dn. iv. 10ff.

security? Was not Campbell Morgan right when he wrote: 'Men have attempted by manipulation of material things to make of Christianity a great imperial power.' 'Wherever the Church has risen to anything like worldly power it has become a refuge for the things that are unclean and polluting and life-destructive.'[1]

Our Lord followed this parable of the mustard seed by saying:

> The kingdom of heaven is like unto leaven, which a woman took, and hid in three measures of meal, till the whole was leavened.[2]

Here, in contrast to the popular idea of its meaning, the understanding and interpretation of this parable are revolutionized if one recognizes in the addition of the leaven the admixture of an evil influence to something otherwise very good without it. There are very strong scriptural grounds for adopting such a view. Whenever leaven is used symbolically elsewhere in the Bible, it represents evil influence. What is more, in several places in the Old Testament 'three measures of meal' (i.e. an *ephah*) constitute an offering made to God Himself. What the Scriptures emphasize is that such an offering was, and had to be, unleavened.[3]

Our Lord's parable, therefore, suggests the improper introduction of leaven by a woman, who can obviously be taken to symbolize household management. In addition, our Lord more than once used leaven elsewhere in His teaching to symbolize influences of which He exhorted His disciples to beware. And He indicated that these influences were exercised by those leaders in Israel who dominated the life and practice of men by their teaching and their religious ceremonialism which our Lord called hypocrisy or 'play acting'. Let us quote what the Scriptures record:

> Then Jesus said unto them, Take heed and beware of the leaven of the Pharisees and of the Sadducees. And they reasoned among themselves, saying, It is because we have taken no bread. Which

[1] *The Parables of the Kingdom*, pp. 90, 91
[2] Mt. xiii. 33; cf. Lk. xiii. 20, 21
[3] See Gn. xviii. 6–8; Lv. ii. 4, 11; Jdg. vi. 19; 1 Sa. i. 24

> when Jesus perceived, he said unto them, O ye of little faith, . . . How is it that ye do not understand that I spake it not to you concerning bread, that ye should beware of the leaven of the Pharisees and of the Sadducees? Then understood they how that he bade them not beware of the leaven of bread, but of the doctrine (RV, teaching) of the Pharisees and of the Sadducees.[1] He began to say unto his disciples first of all, Beware ye of the leaven of the Pharisees, which is hypocrisy.[2]

Similarly, when St. Paul was warning the Galatian Christians against the dangers to their faith and life in Christ of the legalism and ceremonialism which Judaizing teachers were striving to introduce, he said:

> Ye did run well; who did hinder you that ye should not obey the truth? This persuasion cometh not of him that calleth you. A little leaven leaveneth the whole lump.[3]

Thus understood, these two parables of our Lord and their teaching have obvious modern relevance. They describe the situation in which many Christians find themselves. For, during the last hundred years, two evil influences, introduced and exercised by the household management or ruling elders, have increasingly disturbed, perverted, and corrupted local church life. One is the re-introduction of unscriptural claims and practice in connection with the function of the minister and the use of the Lord's supper. In consequence the sacrament given by our Lord to man is turned into a sacrifice to be offered to God; and ministers in the church claim in an exclusive way to be 'priests', in the full sacerdotal sense of the word, and, as such, necessary mediators of grace between God and men. It is asserted, also, that only bishops, in proper apostolic succession through their consecration by other bishops, can ordain such 'priests'; and that without these ministers functioning in this way the true Church does not exist.

The other influence has been scientific and rationalistic. Consequent upon modern liberal criticism, faith in the Bible as the authoritative God-given Word has been undermined. Those who have been most exposed to these dangers have

[1] Mt. xvi. 6–8, 11, 12 [2] Lk. xii. 1 [3] Gal. v. 7–9

been ministers-to-be during the course of their college training. In consequence, the whole Bible is not preached and taught from our pulpits and in our churches in the way that it ought to be. The radical character and the far-reaching extent of the consequent damage to spiritual life and to moral standards are inadequately realized. The whole lump of Church life has been grievously leavened.

The result is a distressing situation, to which official church leaders seem blind, or which they seem unwilling to recognize and to face as they ought. For, in many places, there are genuine believers in our Lord, not a few of them comparatively recent converts, born-again of God's Spirit, souls with a God-given spiritual discernment and appetite, who find that in many local churches either they are offered, by one who claims to be a 'priest', ministries which they rightly regard as unscriptural; or they are not given from the pulpit, or elsewhere during the week, the explicit Bible preaching and teaching which they hungrily desire. This desire is the more insistent, and those possessed by it are the more unwilling to be put off by unworthy substitutes, because they have proved in experience that it is the Scriptures that the Spirit of God uses to give men needed light and food for worthy Christian living. Nor, on the other hand, is there much indication that church authorities are alive to this situation, and eager to remedy it. Rather, many seem determined to perpetuate it by seeing, as far as they can, that ministers-to-be during their training are conformed to the prevailing types, by being made, if possible, more sympathetic towards unscriptural 'priestly' pretensions, and more submissive to damaging biblical criticism.

It is this situation which has been the cause, and is the explanation, of the emergence of many groups and the regular or occasional holding of many meetings, which are independent of the existing local churches. This situation is at least partly responsible also for the widespread and world-wide growth during the last hundred years of local meetings of Brethren, whose missionary activity is now said to exceed in quantity that of any other so-called 'denomination'. In Great Britain the largest fresh growth of a denominational kind has been that of a fellowship which significantly calls itself the Fellowship of Independent Evangelical Churches. This is a group of churches which confessedly regards unity in the Spirit and loyalty to the truth of the gospel as more essential to vital local church life than elaborate, and at times dangerous, denominational integration, which can so easily give greater organizational efficiency and better financial conditions only at the cost of spiritual purity and vitality.

God's blessing has unquestionably rested upon these new movements. His Spirit is at work among them. Yet the big denominational groups, whose members often wrongly use the word 'Church' to describe such a closely-integrated organization of local churches, tend to refuse to recognize these movements and those blessed in them as belonging to the Church of God at all. They are so wedded to the 'big tree' idea of the Church that they can find no place for unpretentious plants. Yet it is the faith and the life possessed by these movements that are essential to the very existence of the Church in a way that particular forms of Church order and government are not.

That which, more than anything else, would bring back to Great Britain a widespread revival of true local church life and fruitfulness within the existing denominations would be the giving to local churches of ministers who, without unscriptural sacerdotalism and sacramentalism, would preach the gospel and shepherd the flock of God; and who, without being diverted by philosophy and scientific criticism, would teach from all the Scriptures the whole counsel of God. Which may God grant.

IV. THE GOAL IN VIEW

CHAPTER TWELVE

BEHOLD, THE BRIDEGROOM COMETH

WE cannot properly conclude this survey of biblical teaching concerning the people of God without recognizing that the best is yet to be. The crowning consummation lies beyond this present life. There is no scriptural justification for expecting complete fulfilment here and now. For our present experience of salvation in Christ and by the Spirit, however genuine and wonderful, is nevertheless incomplete. We still live in bodies that are frail and liable to decay and corruption. We still have by natural birth an old nature that is sinful. We still live in a world in which evil is very active.

Not only so, the very Christian community to which we belong is one in which genuine and nominal, good and bad, are inevitably mixed. Here in this life no absolutely perfect achievement is possible, either in personal Christian holiness or in corporate Christian fellowship, although, of course, we should always be striving in both these matters to approach nearer to the goal.

We must remember also that in any one generation the living Church militant here on earth consists of only a small minority of the full membership of the redeemed people of God. If, as the New Testament declares, the Old Testament saints could not be made perfect without New Testament Christians,[1] no more can we, the present generation of Christians on earth, realize perfection except in the full company and communion of all the saints. In the crowning fulfilment, which our Lord foretold, and which the inspired writers of Scripture visualize, we must 'sit down with Abraham, and Isaac, and Jacob'.[2] We must be 'before the throne, and before the Lamb' part of an innumerable multitude 'of all nations, and kindreds, and people, and tongues'.[3]

[1] See Heb. xi. 39, 40 [2] Mt. viii. 11 [3] Rev. vii. 9

Or again, just as the Church of Christ began only in Christ risen from the dead,[1] just as all who truly belong to it are joined to the risen and enthroned Lord in heavenly places[2] and are sharers by the Spirit in a new creation which is not of this present natural order, so the Church will enjoy the complete consummation of its destiny only when the bodies of the saints and the world in which they live are alike made new.

Such fulfilments are for the people of God all part of the goal in view; they are all part of the purpose of God for His people. They are to occur, so the Scriptures make it plain, when the heavenly Bridegroom comes to claim His Bride, and to bid His people sit down with Him at the marriage feast. Then, by His coming in power and glory, He will complete the salvation of His people for whom He once came in humility to die a death of shame. 'So', we read, 'Christ was once offered to bear the sins of many; and unto them that look for him shall he appear the second time without (RV, 'apart from') sin unto salvation.'[3]

This certain and rewarding consequence of Christ's own earthly sacrifice of Himself for sins is also doubly affirmed in the significant series of seven parables[4] to which we have already referred in the previous chapter. The first four parables, of the sower, the wheat and the tares, the mustard seed, and the leaven, were all spoken to the multitude. They give an outside view of the apparent fortunes of the affairs of the kingdom. But after Jesus had sent the multitude away and had gone indoors with His disciples,[5] He shared with them a complementary inside understanding, by which He made them aware that, in spite of poor response, active opposition and unwelcome perversion, a sure, worth-while result would be gained.

Let us then consider in particular two more of these parables.

> Again, the kingdom of heaven is like unto treasure hid in a field; the which when a man hath found, he hideth, and for joy thereof goeth and selleth all that he hath, and buyeth that field.

[1] See Col. i. 18 [2] See Eph. ii. 6 [3] Heb. ix. 28
[4] See Mt. xiii [5] See Mt. xiii. 36ff.

> Again, the kingdom of heaven is like unto a merchant man, seeking goodly pearls: who, when he had found one pearl of great price, went and sold all that he had, and bought it.[1]

Admittedly many interpret these parables differently. But if we follow the symbolism already adopted in the earlier parables, namely, that the field is the world, and that the man at work in it with a view to gaining something from it is the Son of man, then we must acknowledge that Christ is here indicating that from the world,—though for a period by His own deliberate action its presence will be hidden,—He is going ultimately to secure for Himself, and to unearth for all to see, a worth-while treasure, a treasure which is further represented in the following parable, which reiterates the same truth, as a pearl of great price.

It is this sure reward which will be gained thereby, that will make our Lord's supreme sacrifice of Himself worth while. In other words, to adopt the prophetic language of Isaiah concerning Jehovah's suffering servant, Jesus knew that He would 'see of the travail of his soul, and . . . be satisfied'.[2] And St. Paul says explicitly later that it is the Church for which Christ in love gave Himself, 'that he might present it to himself a glorious church, not having spot, or wrinkle, or any such thing'.[3]

In the New Testament Epistles this consummation of being openly possessed by Christ as His own is explicitly set before believers as a sure prospect, an experience to be enjoyed by all who are truly citizens of the heavenly Zion when the Lord comes for His own. Let us then consider some of the important scriptural statements concerning this fulfilment that we may appreciate what its main features are to be.

First, the Lord Himself will re-appear. As the man who sowed the good seed in the field of the world, He will come back to the same field to reap the harvest.[4] Notice what He Himself said:

> The harvest is the end of the world. The Son of man shall send

[1] Mt. xiii. 44–46 [2] Is. liii. 11 [3] See Eph. v. 25–27
[4] See Mt. xiii. 37, 38, 40, 41; Mk. iv. 26–29

> forth his angels, and they shall gather out of his kingdom all things that offend, and them which do iniquity; and shall cast them into a furnace of fire.[1] And he shall send his angels with a great sound of a trumpet, and they shall gather together his elect from the four winds, from one end of heaven to the other.[2]

Until the Lord Himself thus appears in person, and sends forth His angels to separate bad from good, the present mixture within the visible earthly community must continue. This truth is illustrated and emphasized by the seventh and last of the parables which our Lord told as a coherent series, the parable of the dragnet.[3] This plainly teaches, first, that during the present age the visible company gathered through the preaching of the gospel will inevitably be mixed in character, and second, that the necessary separation of 'the wicked from among the just' will be performed by the angels 'at the end of the world' (or 'consummation of the age').

The same truth, that separation between the genuine and the nominal will take place when the Bridegroom comes, is confirmed in the parable of the marriage feast. There we are told that 'when the king came in to see the guests', the first thing He did was Himself to turn out a would-be guest, who was unprepared for the feast, and who, when interrogated, was speechless in self-defence.

> Then said the king to the servants, Bind him hand and foot, and take him away, and cast him into outer darkness.[4]

Next, when the Lord thus re-appears He will complete His reign and His victory by triumphing over the last enemy, death,[5] and by giving to all His people glorified resurrection bodies. For, in His own resurrection from the grave as the triumphant man, He was 'the firstfruits' of the final harvest. Then 'at his coming they that are Christ's' will also be raised or transfigured to share His glory.[6] So St. Paul writes:

> For our citizenship is in heaven; from whence also we wait for a Saviour, the Lord Jesus Christ: who shall fashion anew the

[1] Mt. xiii. 39, 41, 42
[2] Mt. xxiv. 31
[3] See Mt. xiii. 47–50; and RV mg.
[4] See Mt. xxii. 1–14
[5] See 1 Cor. xv. 25, 26
[6] 1 Cor. xv. 20–23, 51–54

body of our humiliation, that it may be conformed to the body of his glory, according to the working whereby he is able even to subject all things unto himself.[1]

Similarly St. John writes:

Beloved, now are we the sons of God, and it doth not yet appear what we shall be: but we know that, when he shall appear, we shall be like him; for we shall see him as he is.[2]

St. Paul also explains that the generation of Christians who are alive on the earth when this occurs will not die, but that they will simultaneously share in the same bodily glorification. This glorification is necessary, because our present corruptible bodies of flesh and blood cannot inherit the incorruptible kingdom of God.[3] So St. Paul declares:

Behold, I shew you a mystery; We shall not all sleep, but we shall all be changed, in a moment, in the twinkling of an eye, at the last trump: for the trumpet shall sound, and the dead shall be raised incorruptible, and we shall be changed. For this corruptible must put on incorruption, and this mortal must put on immortality.[4]

Also, because this completion of redemption concerns the body, and involves a change of the kind of body all have in this world, and because the departed saints, whose spirits are already with Christ, have left their earthly bodies behind them here in the grave, this consummation for dead and living alike is represented as an experience of being caught up from the earth, and things earthy, to meet the Lord in the air, and thenceforth to be for ever with the Lord. Again, to quote St. Paul:

For the Lord himself shall descend from heaven with a shout, with the voice of the archangel, and with the trump of God: and the dead in Christ shall rise first: then we which are alive and remain shall be caught up together with them in the clouds, to meet the Lord in the air: and so shall we ever be with the Lord.[5]

On the other hand, because in the Spirit all who are truly in Christ, whether departed or still on earth, are to be thought

[1] Phil. iii. 20, 21, RV
[2] 1 Jn. iii. 2
[3] See 1 Cor. xv. 50
[4] 1 Cor. xv. 51–53
[5] 1 Thes. iv. 16, 17

of as already 'in heavenly places' as citizens of the heavenly Jerusalem, the consummation is also represented as a coming down from above. Recording his vision, St. John writes:

> And I John saw the holy city, new Jerusalem, coming down from God out of heaven, prepared as a bride adorned for her husband.[1]

It is also noteworthy in this same connection that, in the passage previously quoted about the dead and the living being caught up from the earth, St. Paul says of the spirits of the departed that they will come down with Jesus from above.

> For if we believe that Jesus died and rose again, even so them also which sleep in Jesus will God bring with him.[2]

This means, finally, that the scene of the consummation will be in the air or heavens, where the clouds are, and on the earth. Yet it will not be this present world just as it now is. For Christ Himself predicted, in connection with His second coming, that 'heaven and earth shall pass away'.[3] St. Peter in his second Epistle, when he refers to 'the promise of his coming', repeats the same prediction:

> But the day of the Lord will come as a thief in the night; in the which the heavens shall pass away with a great noise, and the elements shall melt with fervent heat, the earth also and the works that are therein shall be burned up.[4]

What the people of God are to look for, 'according to his promise' is 'new heavens and a new earth, wherein dwelleth righteousness'.[5] This prospect St. John also confirms. For before he describes seeing the 'new Jerusalem, coming down from God out of heaven', he writes:

> And I saw a new heaven and a new earth: for the first heaven and the first earth were passed away.[6]

St. Paul goes into greater detail on this subject. He says the present world order is like a woman in labour pains, waiting for the hour of liberation. Out of the old order the new will be born, and the crowning event of that day for which the whole creation yearns will be 'the manifestation of the sons

[1] Rev. xxi. 2 [2] 1 Thes. iv. 14 [3] Mt. xxiv. 35
[4] 2 Pet. iii. 4, 10 [5] 2 Pet. iii. 13 [6] Rev. xxi. 1

of God'.[1] For not only is Christ then to be revealed in glory for all to see, but also His glory, as St. Paul says, is to be 'revealed to us-ward'[2] or upon us. He and we are to be 'glorified together'.[3] So all the universe will then know, as they do not know now, who belongs to God's family. Indeed, the new liberty 'from the bondage of corruption' of the whole created order will be a deliverance granted and enjoyed as the promised heritage of God's people—'the glorious liberty of the children of God'.[4] Thus in the ages to come God's grace and power will be yet more glorified in the Church than they are now.[5]

It is, therefore, supremely important that true Christians should live in hope.[6]

> For here have we no continuing city, but we seek one to come.[7] If in this life only we have hope in Christ, we are of all men most miserable (or 'pitiable').[8]

Life in this world is, for Christians, like a journey through the wilderness, between Egypt and Canaan, between the bondage which we have left behind and the promised inheritance to which we are going. This world is like a workshop or school in which God fashions and disciplines His people. The present visible community or professing Church is like the womb out of which the true Church is born, or like the mother by whom the sons of God are nurtured. But the heritage belongs to the true children of God who are thus born and brought up, just as it was the children born in the wilderness who entered Canaan rather than the generation which came out of Egypt by Moses (except, of course, for the true men of faith).

Entrance into the promised land of resurrection glory, like the ancient crossing of Jordan into Canaan, is, in the crowning fulfilment of 'the resurrection of the body', something God's people will do all together, when the number of His elect is complete. It is they who constitute 'the church of the firstborn who are enrolled in heaven'.[9] They are

[1] See Rom. viii. 17–23 [2] See Rom. viii. 18, RV [3] Rom. viii. 17
[4] Rom. viii. 21 [5] See Eph. ii. 7, iii. 20, 21 [6] See Rom. viii. 24, 25
[7] Heb. xiii. 14 [8] 1 Cor. xv. 19 and RV
[9] Heb. xii. 23, RV

the called according to his purpose. For whom he did foreknow, he also did predestinate to be conformed to the image of his Son, that he might be the firstborn among many brethren.[1]

And after these things I heard a great voice of much people in heaven, saying, Alleluia; Salvation, and glory, and honour, and power, unto the Lord our God.

Let us be glad and rejoice, and give honour to him: for the marriage of the Lamb is come, and his wife hath made herself ready.

And he saith unto me, Write, Blessed are they which are called unto the marriage supper of the Lamb.[2]

And I heard a great voice out of the heaven saying, Behold, the tabernacle of God is with men, and he will dwell with them, and they shall be his people, and God himself shall be with them, and be their God.[3]

[1] Rom. viii. 28, 29 [2] Rev. xix. 1, 7, 9 [3] Rev. xxi. 3